bcpusa.org

The Journey of a Lifetime 1

From This Day Forward

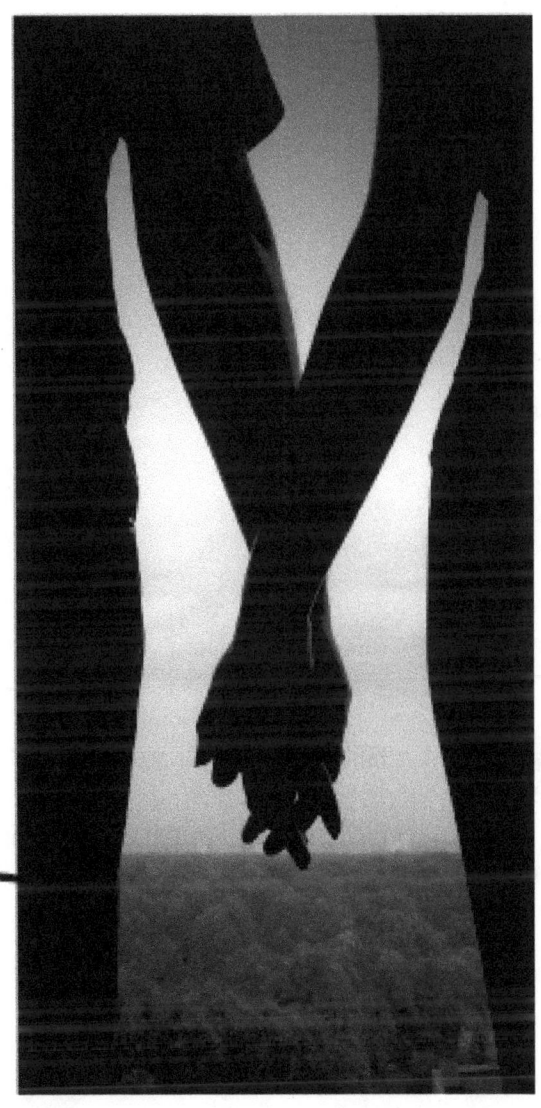

Preparing Couples for the Journey of a Lifetime

Counselor's Edition

Dr. Michael J. Peck

All Scripture quotations are from the Authorized King James Version of the Holy Bible.

ISBN 978-1-936285-01-3

Published by Baptist Church Planters
36830 Royalton Road
Grafton, Ohio 44044

440-748-1677

Web Site: www.bcpusa.org
Email: bcp@bcpusa.org

© Baptist Church Planters 2010

Designed by an idea—anideaweb.com

A Word from the Author

From This Day Forward—Preparing Couples for the Journey of a Lifetime is a premarital counseling manual more than three decades in the making. Working with couples as they begin a new home and family is a great privilege. It is also a great responsibility. What a great opportunity the counseling pastor has in preparing the way not only for the couple, but for the generations to come!

Use this handbook in addition to the couple's edition in two different ways. First, the counseling pastor who wishes to use this book for his entire premarital counseling model may be assured he is preparing well the couple for marriage, home and family. **Note: For maximum effectiveness, in addition to the Counselor's edition, be sure to use *From This Day Forward—Preparing Couples for the Journey of a Lifetime (Couple's edition)*. Before every counseling session, the Couple's edition assigns work that is practical and biblical to be completed in anticipation of your next counseling appointment. In each chapter, compare the work they are to complete with the counseling material you will present as well as your own notes.**

Every area of the premarital counseling program is addressed in tests and assignments that are easy to follow, practical and pointedly biblical. Found in their entirety in Chapter 14, these same tests are also repeated section by section in the appropriate counseling sessions. For the counseling pastor, these tests are both uncomplicated and yet sufficiently thorough to aid in the counseling process. Creative and specific biblical counseling will be the outflow of these assignments for the counselor using this handbook as his model.

The second way this handbook may be used is to view the material as being supplemental. For those counseling pastors who already have their counseling models in use, this book contains information, testing and assignments that may be added to counseling programs already in place. A wide margin is used throughout the handbook. This provides ample opportunity for the counseling pastor to add his own notes, Scripture references and illustrations.

Additional resources make this handbook particularly useful. Three brand new wedding ceremonies are included in Chapter 7, and many suggestions for making the ceremony truly unique are offered in Chapter 8. Additional counseling aids and worksheets are made available in Chapter 13.

Whether you are beginning your counseling ministry or even if you have been preparing couples for many years, it is my prayer that this handbook will be helpful to you as a counseling pastor, as well as beneficial to couples who are ready to begin their journey of a lifetime.

Michael J. Peck, D.Min.

Acknowledgements

A very special thank you goes to my dear wife Karen. She is my best friend. Her faithful walk with the Lord, her love for me, and her commitment to our marriage make writing a premarital counseling handbook not only possible, but a joy.

To my friend and editor, Robert Bowker, a sincere thank you is extended. His contribution to this book is hard to describe. Bob's expertise in editing is invaluable, and his suggestions are excellent. You are a faithful partner in ministry, Bob.

To a good friend of the ministry of Baptist Church Planters, Mrs. Davina Allgrim, I offer a sincere note of thanks for reading the manuscript and making many suggestions. Your time and insight are a blessing to us.

To my friend, Lawrence Montgomery, thank you for the hours you invested on the manuscript. Your suggestions are so appreciated.

Thanks also to my pastor, Rev. Noel Hack, for reading the manuscript from the pastor's viewpoint. His encouragement is very special.

Lastly, thank you to my dear family and friends who kept praying and encouraging me to write *From This Day Forward*. Your partnership continues to be an incredible blessing. You will never know how much your prayers have helped me in this project.

****

For maximum effectiveness use this resource along with *From This Day Forward-Preparing Couples for the Journey of a Lifetime Couple's Edition*. This will complement your counseling edition as well as provide specific encouragement to the couple.

Contents

From This Day Forward

Preparing Couples for the Journey of a Lifetime

Introduction Just Between Us 1

Chapter 1—Counseling Session 1
Foundations for Every Couple..7

Chapter 2—Counseling Session 2
Let the Journey Begin..13

Chapter 3—Counseling Session 3
A Great Marriage- Settle for Nothing Less 18

Chapter 4—Counseling Session 4
My View of Home and Marriage 27

Chapter 5—Counseling Session 5
Making a Marriage that Works and Grows 35

Chapter 6—Counseling Session 6
The Goal and Joy of Intimacy 47

Chapter 7—Counseling Session 7
Helping the Couple Plan Their Special Day 56

Chapter 8—Special Features
Making the Ceremony Unique 71

Chapter 9—The Reception
A Time of Celebration...80

Chapter 10—Suggested Timeline
Countdown to the Wedding 82

Chapter 11—Financial Guidelines
Who Pays for What in the Wedding and Reception? 85

Chapter 12—The Postwedding Follow-up Counseling Session
The Couple and Their Adjustments 86

Chapter 13—Supplemental Worksheets and Additional Counseling Aids............92

Chapter 14—The Tests and Assignments..102

Contents

From This Day Forward

Preparing Couples for the Journey of a Lifetime

Introduction Just Between Us 1

Chapter 1—Counseling Session 1
Foundations for Every Couple..7

Chapter 2—Counseling Session 2
Let the Journey Begin...13

Chapter 3—Counseling Session 3
A Great Marriage- Settle for Nothing Less 18

Chapter 4—Counseling Session 4
My View of Home and Marriage 27

Chapter 5—Counseling Session 5
Making a Marriage that Works and Grows 35

Chapter 6—Counseling Session 6
The Goal and Joy of Intimacy 47

Chapter 7—Counseling Session 7
Helping the Couple Plan Their Special Day 56

Chapter 8—Special Features
Making the Ceremony Unique 71

Chapter 9—The Reception
A Time of Celebration...80

Chapter 10—Suggested Timeline
Countdown to the Wedding 82

Chapter 11—Financial Guidelines
Who Pays for What in the Wedding and Reception?..................................85

Chapter 12—The Postwedding Follow-up Counseling Session
The Couple and Their Adjustments 86

Chapter 13—Supplemental Worksheets and Additional Counseling Aids............92

Chapter 14—The Tests and Assignments...102

Introduction

Just Between Us

A few matters of the heart just between you, me, and the Lord!
Getting Ready for Premarital Counseling.

The Man behind the Desk

As a pastor, you daily face at least two wonderful and incredible things. These two things come bundled as (1) opportunities and (2) responsibilities. Every day most pastors sense the incredible responsibility of the office. In your "busyness" don't forget the wonderful opportunities God has given you. When you began to sense the call of God upon your life (1 Timothy 3:1), you knew it would be a "good work." However, it probably did not take too long to discover the magnitude of this good work. For me, the full impact of the ministry began to register when my first funeral came. Then my first appointment for premarital counseling was scheduled. Did I ever need the Lord's direction and help! I still do.

Many pastors know that the Lord has given them a huge opportunity when a couple schedules an appointment for premarital counseling. More than just a few pastors feel inadequate to counsel and unprepared to really help the couple establish a home that will last a lifetime. If you experience the mixed emotions of joy and apprehension, excitement and yet the overwhelming sense that this responsibility is huge, rest assured-you are not alone.

Before the couple arrives, let's share privately and honestly together as pastors. Though today I serve as the vice president of Baptist Church Planters, I still have a pastor's heart. From thirty-one years of being the pastor of dear churches in the state of New York, I know how pastors think and how they view the role of being the pastor-counselor. It is a weighty matter, isn't it? Brother, rest assured that God has called you to a good work as you invest in this couple. You are not responsible for the way they will build (or not build) their marriage. You are only responsible for preparing them as much as possible.

> Have you thought about these two words lately?
> **Good**= *kalos* (kal-OS) meaning that which is "Beautiful, handsome, excellent, precious."
> **Work**= *ergon* (ER-gon) meaning, "That which one undertakes to do, anything accomplished by the hand."
> May the Lord keep your ministry fresh in your heart so that you can view it as that "good work."

Five Matters to Keep Fresh

As pastors there are five things we must ever keep before us in premarital counseling situations. These five things help to keep me on track and focused as I balance between my opportunities and my responsibilities.

> You may keep current with the US Census statistical information at www.census.gov/

I must be CONCERNED about the condition of marriages

It is no secret that American homes and families have great needs. The traditional family (one daddy-one mommy for a lifetime, with the children having the same last name) now accounts for only 25% of the homes in the United States. Homes and families are undergoing huge changes as more and more single daddies are raising children. Over 500,000 children are being raised in foster care throughout our country. Marriages are ending in tragic divorces nearly 50% of the time.

Your schedule is certainly full, but the Lord will help you to manage your time as you prepare this couple for marriage. Do not think this is time that could be better invested. You and pastors like you are standing firm because of godly concern for marriages. Your conviction will be demonstrated as you share biblical principles with passion, urgency, and tenderness. The couple will sense the sincerity of your ministry because of your concern for them.

I must be CONFIDENT in the Lord and His Word

While it will be important for the couple to read several good books concerning marriage and family living, nothing can compare to the Word of God. God's Word is likened to a lamp (Psalm 119:105), fire (Jeremiah 5:14), a hammer (Jeremiah 23:29), seed (Matthew 13:18-23), and a sword (Ephesians 6:17). These pictures speak of God's Word being useful and practical for daily living. How amazing that God would breathe His Word (2 Timothy 3:16)! No wonder the Apostle Paul declares that the Word is "…profitable for doctrine, for reproof, for correction, for instruction in righteousness: That the man of God may be perfect, throughly furnished unto all good works" (2 Timothy 3:16b-17). This includes the state of marriage and home!

Throughout the premarital counseling process, *From This Day Forward* will provide you with abundant scripture references and direction to help each couple prepare for marriage. You will also be able to develop and implement your own areas of scriptural counsel. The Lord is the creator of the marriage institution, and His Word provides the clear instructions for successful and blessed marital living. You may always rest confident in the power of the Word of God.

I must be CONSISTENT in being an example

I am thankful that the pastor and his wife do not have to be perfect! Sometimes an unreasonable person in the congregation may try to hold us to that unattainable standard; however, the Lord does not demand perfection. Do not expect a state of perfection from your mate. Do not demand it of yourself.

On the other hand, never hide behind the excuse of "only being human" as a license for a poor marriage. The Bible clearly addresses the standard for the marriage of the pastor and his wife in 1 Timothy 3:2. The standard is impressive as Paul writes, "A bishop then must be blameless, the husband of one wife…" The idea of "blameless" is being above reproach. There must not be a glaring pattern of habitually repeated misconduct.

The pastor must live in a way that makes it difficult to bring about a charge against him. Through the Lord's help and grace, blameless (not perfect) living is achieved.

Sidebar notes:

Think of it, 75% of the families that visit your church are non-traditional. They will come having been married two or more times. Children from one family will be enrolled in your Sunday school with two or three different last names.

Rather than despairing, view this as a great opportunity for teaching and discipleship. Think about developing a Bible basics class on marriage and home.

Two verses often encouraged me when preparing for any counseling situation. They were 1 Kings 8:56 and Isaiah 55:11.

Successful counseling is providing the scripture and watching God do the work.

Wise pastors, though they handle the Word daily, never lose the sense of awe at God's Word. "…My heart stands in awe of thy word" (Psalm 119:161). In our own personal life the Word must be our standard of conduct (Titus 2:15), source of joy (Psalm 119:162), and spiritual food (1 Peter 2:2).

Peter strongly reminded pastors that they must be an example to the flock (1 Peter 5:3). Without drawing attention to your wife and marriage, by the grace of God, make it a marriage that others could easily model.

Paul's writing to Timothy concerning the marriage of a bishop far exceeds simply managing to stay married. Literally the thought is to become "a one-woman kind of man." The pastor, through the Lord's enabling, is to set the example of being a man who loves one woman, who lives for one woman, is focused upon the affection of one woman, is fulfilled emotionally and satisfied sexually by one woman-his wife. The blamelessness seems to be the public matter. The "husband of one wife" is accomplished in private with a public manifestation.

Take a moment to think seriously about the pointed admonition of Proverbs 5:15-20.

> "Drink waters out of thine own cistern, and running waters out of thine own well. Let thy fountains be dispersed abroad, and rivers of waters in the streets. Let them be only thine own, and not strangers with thee. Let thy fountain be blessed: and rejoice with the wife of thy youth. Let her be as the loving hind and pleasant roe; let her breasts satisfy thee at all times; and be thou ravished always with her love. And why wilt thou, my son, be ravished with a strange woman, and embrace the bosom of a stranger?"

When you are "ravished" with the love of your wife, you will have safeguards well established, a marriage that is fresh, an intimacy that is growing and vibrant, as well as a ministry that is confirmed by the fact that you as the pastor are living in your home what you are preaching at church! This honest and genuine love in your marriage will be a great encouragement and profound enhancement in your ministry. Remember, this type of marriage does not flaunt itself. It does not boast or brag. It simply radiates the genuine and quiet love that Christ can build in the lives of two people who are fully committed to Him and to each other.

I must be CONVINCED of the importance of my investment

Most people are not aware of the commitment and involvement that goes into counseling. Those who never counsel give little thought to the preparation for the session, the time involved during the session, and the energy that is exhausted conducting the session. Wise pastors who handle the Word of God in the privacy of their office through pastoral counseling must be convinced that their efforts are worthwhile.

Sometimes the results of the Word of God in the life of a person come quickly and dramatically. I have witnessed those who make a decision which brings about immediate changes because of the biblical application from the counseling session. Quite frankly, those times seemed to be the exception to the rule, not the typical. Often, counseling was more like the proverbial planting the seed, watering it consistently, carefully weeding out that which is harmful and then waiting for the results to begin to show. Neither harvest nor counselees often are rushed!

I must be CONTENT to be the Lord's servant

Good servants remember this blessed fact, "I am not in charge. My Master is the boss. The Lord owns His church and He is building it." This does not diminish our responsibility to be faithful. However, it does free us from our self-imposed expectations that often are nearly impossible to achieve.

Ten Principles for Purity from Proverbs 5:

1. Exercise great caution (5:1-2).

2. Temptation usually presents itself in an attractive manner (5:3).

3. Be on guard for the power of persuasive words (5:3).

4. While the temptation may appear attractive, remember that the sure consequences will be bitter (5:4-5).

5. To flirt with the possibility is a dangerous road (5:6).

6. Develop the right convictions, standards and policies. Be committed to staying as far from the temptation as possible (5:7-8).

7. Always remember the fact that twenty minutes of passion is never worth the twenty years of pain (5:9-14).

8. Do my part to keep my marriage beautiful (5:15-17).

9. Grow in my love and devotion to my mate (5:15-20).

10. Heed the warning of the Lord (5:21-23).

Introduction

Several principles continue to be a blessing and encouragement to me in the pastoral counseling ministry. Among the many things we could share, these wonderful truths have sustained and helped me.

1. I am not responsible for results. Many pastors are "results driven" in every area of ministry and personal life. While we must never be lazy, it is imperative to remember that only God can bring about results.
2. Though I deeply care about the counselees, they do not belong to me. With affection some pastors refer to the congregation as "my people" or "my flock" and while that is tender and personal, it is not accurate. I need to remember that these precious believers belong to the Lord Jesus. The price He paid for them is incredible (1 Corinthians 6:19-20). Do not allow yourself to fall into the trap that somehow this counselee is your personal responsibility.
3. Christ has promised that He will build His church. It has always been my personal conviction that biblical pastoral counseling is actually discipleship in progress. Christ's promise to build His church applies to quantity through evangelism as well as quality through discipleship. While we are privileged to be used of the Lord in discipleship and counseling, it is exciting and encouraging to remember that the One who owns His church is none other than the Builder, the Lord Jesus Himself.
4. I cannot make people change. A profound statement is proclaimed in Jeremiah 17:9-10. "The heart is deceitful above all things, and desperately wicked: who can know it? I the LORD search the heart…" There are times that the pastor-counselor is grieved because of the hardness of the heart attitude manifested in the session. No amount of coaxing, reasoning, pleading, threatening or nagging can change the human heart. Take the pressure off yourself by remembering that only the Lord can change the human heart.
5. I am required to be faithful in pleasing the Lord. Through the grace of the Lord Jesus Christ, I can be faithful to Him. He is the One to whom I am ultimately responsible. He is the One that I must please. He is the One that best understands me and knows my motives and desires. Pastor, you are not a miracle worker; but you serve One who is! As you serve Him because of His love for you and your love for Him, handle His Word carefully, accurately, appropriately and consistently. He will be pleased.

> Have you ever preached a series of topical messages on the word "heart" as found in the Psalms? It is a rich study with practical applications.

Set the goal of pleasing the Lord throughout each part of the counseling session. As you work through the situations with the couple as relating to their backgrounds and views, always bring them to the decision point of seeking to please the Lord. When it comes to the wedding ceremony, be sure it is one that is pleasing to the Lord. Even in the discussion and planning of the reception, honeymoon and early married life, challenge the couple to please the Lord.

Each pastor will have specific standards and policies concerning whom he will consider marrying. Each pastor and local church will incorporate these standards into the premarital counseling sessions. Before the first session, you may wish to ask the couple to fill out the form, "Information Intake-Introducing Ourselves." This will give you the opportunity to get to know the counseling couple better.

The various forms and assignments are found in their entirety in Chapter Fourteen. To assist you in preparing and conducting the counseling sessions, the tests or portions of the tests and assignments used for the particular session will also be found in the chapter.

It is advisable that both the bride and groom each purchase the couple's edition in that it contains helpful principles and each of the tests and assignments as they prepare for marriage. Also, it will complement your edition as well as counseling sessions. They may wish to copy their tests and assignments to submit to you rather than tearing them from their edition. May the Lord bless you, Pastor, as you work with this couple From This Day Forward.

Information Intake—*Introducing Ourselves*

Bride's Information:

Bride's full name _____

Address _____

Date of birth _____ Home phone _____

Cell phone _____

Status: Is this your first marriage? _____

Are you a member of a local church? _____

Name of church _____

Family background:

Names of parents _____

Names and ages of siblings _____

_____

Do you have a personal relationship with the Lord Jesus Christ? _____

If yes, please write a brief paragraph of your testimony of salvation. _____

_____

_____

What are several of the goals for premarital counseling you wish the pastor to emphasize? _____

_____

_____

Are you committed to six (may vary) sessions of premarital counseling
and the completion of homework assignments before each appointment? _____

Date of proposed wedding _____

Location of proposed wedding _____

Groom's Information:

Groom's full name _____

Address _____

Date of birth _____ Home phone _____

Cell phone _____

Status: Is this your first marriage? _____

Are you a member of a local church? _____

Name of church _____

Family background:

Names of parents _____

Names and ages of siblings _____

_____

Do you have a personal relationship with the Lord Jesus Christ? _____

If yes, please write a brief paragraph of your testimony of salvation. _____

_____

_____

What are several of the goals for premarital counseling you wish the pastor to emphasize? _____

_____

_____

Are you committed to six (may vary) sessions of premarital counseling
and the completion of homework assignments before each appointment? _____

6 *From This Day Forward*

Chapter One—Counseling Session 1

Foundations for Every Couple

Even if you are the pastor of this couple and think you know them well, during the next sessions you will get to know this couple as never before. May the Lord give you great wisdom and insight as you prepare this couple for their wedding and married life to follow.

Goals for this Session

1. Share with the couple your joy and the honor that is yours as you counsel them.
2. Review the purpose of premarital counseling.
3. Establish your policies and the necessity of completing homework before each session, as you review the form "Information Intake-Introducing Ourselves."
4. Double-check on the date of the proposed wedding. Make it clear, you are not committing to proceed with the wedding until you are well satisfied they are ready to marry. You may wish to assure them you will hold the date and give them your decision as soon as possible
5. Encourage the couple to commit to becoming the husband and wife the Lord desires, and help them to think about making this a Biblical marriage.

The Couple As They Plan Their Wedding and Married Life

In my three decades of helping couples prepare for their wedding day and married life, I never ceased to be amazed at the process of premarital counseling. Nothing is routine. Every couple comes from a wide variety of backgrounds unique to themselves. Each counselee possesses his or her own level of maturity, spiritual depth (or lack thereof!), personality, expectations and viewpoint.

While *From This Day Forward* will offer a solid biblical course of counseling, every premarital counseling couple will be unique. There are no "cookie-cutter" counseling steps to take with a one-size-fits-all approach. As the counseling pastor, you will need to address specific situations at appropriate times, as well as inserting your specific teaching and application.

The Scriptures provide a beautiful picture of the good shepherd who genuinely knows his sheep. Speaking of the Lord Jesus, the Bible says, "I am the good shepherd, and know my sheep…" (John 10:14). Likewise, good pastor/shepherds know the sheep entrusted to them by the Lord. During these counseling sessions, explain your role to the couple as a shepherd who loves and cares for the sheep. Share with them that

---

Sidebar notes:

Some pastors prefer to require the couple to complete the intake data before they arrive; others give them a few moments to complete the form before the session begins. This is a matter of preference.

There are several reasons for giving homework. First, it gives the couple an opportunity to think through important issues. Second, it provides the counselor the opportunity of seeing areas that need attention. Lastly, it demonstrates the level of commitment the counselees have toward counseling. The next session should not take place until the homework is completed.

Good pastors take seriously Psalm 141:3, "Set a watch, O Lord, before my mouth; keep the door of my lips." Confidentiality is of the utmost priority.

you will be working with them in a precious and personal way. You will become part of some of the most personal and private conversations they will ever share with anyone. Talk often to the Lord about them; but not with anyone else.

Begin the Session

After welcoming the couple and assuring them of your appreciation in sharing this occasion with them, an opening word of prayer seeking the Lord's direction and wisdom is most appropriate.

Share with the couple that it is important to understand why we are engaging in premarital counseling. Some may have the attitude, "I love my fiancé; what else matters?" Explain that love is very important; but to maximize that wonderful love, there are specific goals that need to be achieved during premarital counseling.

> Through this session, the words that are underlined in your handbook will appear as blanks for the couple to fill in throughout their manual.

The Goals of Premarital Counseling

It will be important to remind the couple that every marriage is very important to the Lord and to you as their pastor. Occasionally you will detect that the groom is not convinced that premarital counseling is important. Seldom does the bride seem reluctant. This is an important time to share the purpose and goals of premarital counseling. There are many good reasons to commit to premarital counseling; here are several such reasons to share with the couple. (Remember, the underlined sections are blanks for them to fill in their edition.)

1. Your wedding will be one of the most significant days in your entire life. Premarital counseling is going to facilitate proper planning and preparation.
2. The premarital counseling process will assist the couple to build a truly biblical and meaningful relationship with each other.
3. The premarital counseling time will enable the Lord opportunity to enrich the engagement season for the bridal couple.
4. It will help the couple to discover areas that need to be strengthened or changed before the wedding. Sometimes couples are already aware of such situations, but have concluded that they will wait until after the wedding to address the problems. Then somehow they think they will be able to change their mate. This is not only unwise; it simply does not work.

    Situations needing attention are much better addressed before the wedding. You will have a great opportunity to carefully and prayerfully work through these areas with your couple. Here's a hint to wise pastors: it is better to work through these now than to wait for five or six years when the situation has deteriorated and the marriage is on the verge of fracture.

5. Carefully and honestly working through the premarital counseling process will help to minimize unpleasant surprises after the wedding.
6. The time invested together as the counselor and couple will provide the opportunity to address unnecessary fears as well as answer important questions. The couple has never traveled this road before. From your experience in coun-

> While you probably will not mention the following list to the couple, some of the areas to address in future appointments will focus on dealing with anger, spiritual growth and maturity, unrealistic expectations, poor time management, financial responsibility and communication skills.

> If you have additional goals for the premarital counseling time, feel free to add them at this point. Please mention to the couple that in addition to what the author has shared, you want to add the following.

seling, as well as your own marriage, you will be a great encouragement and a source of helpful information.
7. Always, the Lord Jesus <u>desires that we mature and grow</u> as believers. The days and months before the wedding will be some of the most significant times of their lives. Now is a great time to encourage the couple to consider carefully their spiritual condition. Challenge the couple to become genuine disciples of Christ.

It may seem time-consuming to share all seven of these goals; but actually it is time well invested. Great buildings begin with solid foundations. The foundational goals of premarital counseling must be firmly established for the couple to reap the greatest results.

The Goals of the Couple in Premarital Counseling

At this point, refer to the information intake and note the goals they have listed for premarital counseling. Often this is a reassuring time, as they discover their several goals as being within the focus you have set before them. This is also a good time to ask if they have additional goals to list or questions to ask at this point.

> Counseling pastors vary the length of sessions to fit their schedules. If you are counseling in an extended session, some pastors offer a brief break, have water available and seek to create as relaxed an atmosphere as possible.

Continue the Session

Share with the couple the two things through which we will work in this session. First, we must examine the essential elements of a successful marriage. Second, we must explore four principles to ensure a successful marriage.

Key Words

Ask the couple to turn to Genesis 2:18-24 as you read it.

(Be prepared to provide Bibles unless you requested they bring their own.) After reading this text, remind the couple that we are looking back at the first wedding ceremony and taking note of what the Lord said about the first husband and wife.

How interesting to see that while Adam lived in a paradise, something of significance was missing. "And the LORD God said, It is not good that the man should be alone; I will make him an help meet for him" (2:18). There are several key words to remember.

"Good" (Hebrew word *towb*, pronounced tobe), which means "that which is <u>pleasant, excellent, agreeable</u>." Something very noticeable was missing in Adam's life. God clearly allowed Adam time to discover this. Though he enjoyed the presence of the animal world before they became ferocious, and though he must have been awestruck by fellowship with the Almighty Creator God, something was not good. Adam was alone.

"Alone" (Hebrew word *bad* from *badad*, pronounced baw-DAD), which carries the idea of "<u>separation, being solitary, apartness or existing by one's self.</u>" The aloneness Adam sensed was significant and could not be filled by any of the animals.

"Make" (Hebrew word *asah*, pronounced aw-SAW) which conveys the powerful idea of "to produce, prepare, appoint or bring about."

"Help meet" (Hebrew word *ezer*, pronounced AY-zer) which means to "aid or help in a fully suitable manner." In a truly wonderful way, the Creator designed Eve to be the beautiful complement to and completion of Adam.

How important it is to grasp what the Lord is saying about the first man. In spite of the perfect conditions of Eden and the wonderful fellowship with the Lord, Adam sensed that there was a huge void in his life. He sensed apartness and aloneness in his existence among the animals and even with the Lord. He was not a creature of the fields, waters or air. He certainly was not God. He experienced an acute sense of aloneness, and it was not excellent, agreeable or pleasant.

Thus, the all-wise Creator brought Adam to the point where he was ready for the Lord to produce and bring about the precious and totally suitable complement or helper he needed. What Adam lacked, Eve would provide as Adam's partner. The empty space of aloneness would be incredibly filled with the closeness and intimacy of his wife.

How does this apply to the couple preparing for marriage? Ask the couple to share with you how they apply this to themselves. (You will want to jot these observations down as a possible record to which you may make reference later.)

> It will be interesting for you as a counseling pastor to take note of the ways couples will complement each other in the areas of strengths and weaknesses. How does the "help meet" concept apply to this couple?

After giving time to discuss their observations, it will be essential to address two critical issues. First, she must not be seeking another "daddy" in her husband. Second, he must not be seeking another "mommy" in his wife. Rather, both must seek to become the "help meet" or one who complements and fulfills. The closeness and intimacy of husband and wife is very different from the relationship of parent and child.

> This is a critical moment in the counseling session. Do not assume these things to be true. Ask the Lord for great wisdom and be sensitive as to how they view marriage.
>
> Sometimes individuals feel pressured. Here are a few reasons for this.
> 1. The bride is pregnant.
> 2. All their friends are getting married, and they view this as time is running out.
> 3. Home life is unhappy and this is an escape.
> 4. One or more parents are pushing them into marriage.
> 5. They do not know how to tell their fiancé of their reservations.

Essential Elements of Successful Marriage

Understanding these key words and their application lays a good foundation for the bridal couple. Next, it is imperative to share with them that their marriage must include the following elements.

A sweet confidence (Psalm 40:8)
This confidence comes by knowing this marriage is the will of God for them. Assure the couple that if one or both are not firmly convinced of this, that premarital counseling will be of great assistance in coming to this settled conviction. This is a good time to ask them how they have come to believe this marriage is the will of God for them.

A personal desire (Genesis 24:58)
The bridal couple should be able easily to make the following statements. "I want to marry this person. No one is pressuring me. I am not feeling trapped. I am entering into the wedding and marriage of my own voluntary decision and will."

A lasting pledge or covenant (Matthew 19:6)
This really is "For better or worse…as long as life shall last." Here is a great moment to stress that the word "divorce" must be discarded and removed from their vocabulary. Divorce must never be an option in resolving any problem. This covenant is unconditional.

A daily and consistent investment (Ephesians 5:21)
Daily I give myself to my mate. I am no longer my own. This commitment is powerful and permanent. In every sense, it really is "as long as life shall last."

Four Principles to Insure a Strong Biblical Foundation
It is not sufficient to see the aloneness of Adam and the precious plan for him in the person of Eve; it is also very important for the couple to recognize the four principles to make sure this plan would work for Adam, Eve, and every couple to follow. These principles are not optional. From Genesis 2:24-25, they are essential.

Be leaving (2:24a)
The Hebrew word is *azab* (pronounced aw-ZAB) and has the very strong idea of loosening, letting go, leaving behind. This is not a forsaking of parents, especially in their elderly years. It is rather a loosening of the ties that bind children to their parents. A new tie is to be established, being bound to each other and growing stronger as time goes by.

Be cleaving (2:24b)
The Hebrew word is *dabaq* (pronounced daw-BAK). This word is strongly permanent. It conveys the concept of staying with, being joined with and glued together.

Explore with the couple the concept of "be cleaving." It is important for the couple to grasp that being glued together is both an emotional attachment and a spiritual development. It is far more than sharing an address together. Couples who are "cleaving" grow closer in their relationship over time. This does not happen automatically.

As the couple shares their view of "cleaving," it may be helpful to use the illustration of a marriage bank. Specific acts of love, shared times and experiences, words of appreciation, and daily demonstrations of affection are deposits in the marriage bank. These deposits enhance the bond or the "glue" of cleaving. On the other hand, hurtful, selfish and thoughtless acts are withdrawals and chip away at the cleaving process. Healthy bank accounts and marriages have many more deposits than withdrawals!

Be united (2:24c)
When speaking of "one flesh", the Hebrew concept is beautiful. The word "flesh" is *basar*, (pronounced baw-SAWR) which means kindred, or singular in the sense of closeness.

Explore with the couple several practical applications of the "Be leaving" command.

1. How much do they now depend on their parents for financial support?

2. Do they view financial independence from parents as a matter of maturity and responsibility?

3. Where will they live after their wedding? Explore and emphasize the importance of establishing their own household.

The actual idea of cleaving is to be so bound together that it is impossible to separate without great damage.

Have you ever considered the various levels of interpersonal relationships?

1. Brief encounter- quick hello on the sidewalk.

2. Elevator encounter- several brief comments about the weather or sports.

3. Airline chat- potential for an hour-long conversation, learning about the traveler's family, business, etc.

4. Workplace relationships- This is where you get to know people and their situations.

5. Friendship level- Our friends have seen us in the most trying of times and still choose to love us.

6. Marriage intimacy- nothing compares to this. It is being totally revealed to our mate. It is an honest and loving openness resulting in a closeness that is unparalleled.

Chapter 1

The picture of "one flesh" is a growing closeness, a togetherness that comes through time and walking together. It is a picture of a couple walking so closely that from a distance they appear to be one form rather than two.

Some would chuckle at this. However, those who follow the biblical blueprint for marriage will find the joy of intimacy deepening as the years pass along. Different personalities, various experiences, sudden trials, and even hardships will result in either a widening distance or a growing closeness, depending on the commitment to one flesh made by each couple.

Be totally giving, holding back nothing that is helpful (2:25)

Adam and Eve were naked and not ashamed. In marriage, wise couples hold back everything that will be destructive; but hold back nothing that will be helpful and fulfilling in their relationship.

> As the counseling pastor, add your own personal teaching at this point. Share with the couple several destructive things to hold back as well as helpful things they should do.

These are the goals the Lord has for every marriage of those who know and love Him. Often this is not typical for marriages today. Nevertheless, this is God's standard for a precious marriage. Encourage the couple to establish these goals from this day forward, as the journey of a lifetime is underway.

Conclude the Session

1. Ask if there are any questions about our discussion for today and make any comments you wish to add for this session.
2. The homework entitled "Session 2-Respect and Priority" should be completed and submitted to you at least one week before the next appointment. It will be wise to have the couple make copies of their homework from their premarital counseling edition. This will insure their notes will be kept. Select several verses of Scripture to read, and close in prayer (Psalm 128 is a wonderful choice).

Chapter Two—Counseling Session 2

Let the Journey Begin

Beautiful lawns and healthy bank accounts do not just happen. Likewise, successful and happy marriages do not just happen! Imagine the outcome of a person's lawn if it were left to itself for an entire summer. Not a pretty sight, is it? Beautiful lawns take preparation, fertilization, watering, mowing, trimming, and raking. Let's face it, beautiful lawns require time and effort. Healthy bank accounts require more deposits being invested than withdrawals. It is the same with marriage.

> Do you have several couples that are walking with the Lord and happily married for a number of years? What a dynamic and powerful impact it would be if they could be incorporated into the premarital counseling process. Consider how you could use their testimony of what they did to build a beautiful marriage.

Goals for this Session

1. Help the couple to grasp the importance of understanding each other.
2. Assist the couple in appreciating the importance of their background as relating to respect and priorities.
3. Assess the level of commitment and maturity of the couple as relating to their spiritual lives and the matter of respect and priority for marriage and each other. Do both individuals respect each other enough to prioritize their marriage?

> Couples may find it interesting to see how Isaac obtained his wife. Most will be very thankful marriages are not arranged this way today. The purpose for this reading is to help the couple think through what a home involves and how to grow a beautiful marriage.

Begin the Session

Invite the couple to turn to Genesis 24. It is interesting to note that in the Old Testament period, marriages were arranged by the groom's father. Abraham was old and was blessed by the Lord in his life (verse 1). Knowing the importance of his son marrying the right person, Abraham makes his servant promise he will not take a bride for Isaac from the pagan women who lived nearby.

This chapter stresses the providential way God brought Rebekah to Isaac. Throughout the chapter, God's faithful love is emphasized by the Hebrew word *hesed* which stresses the "loyal love" or "kindness" of the Lord as well as "mercy" (verses 12, 14, 27 and 49).

There are four main divisions to this chapter. As the counseling pastor, you may want to develop these thoughts further or add your personal insights throughout this section.

God's Plan for Isaac and Rebekah

The clear directive given to the servant (24:1-9)
Wonderful lessons concerning God's directions for marriage can be added at this point. Ask the couple for several things to be learned from this.

The powerful dependence expressed by the servant (24:10-27)
The servant prayed very specifically for God's leading. He did not wish to make such a weighty decision based on appearance or convenience. He depended fully upon the Lord for His will and provision. It will be special for the couple to learn to depend fully on the Lord as individuals as well as married partners.

The wonderful discovery of God's answer to the servant (24:28-60)
It is interesting to note the involvement of the family and the blessing they expressed upon the plans. If the family expresses doubt or reservation, it may be worth learning their reasons.

The precious delightfulness of God's provision (24:61-67)
Think of the delightfulness of the words, Isaac "took Rebekah, and she became his wife; and he loved her…" It is a tremendous blessing to enter into such a lifetime commitment and relationship.

Undoubtedly, couples today find the story of a servant finding one's mate, at the direction of the groom's father, to be foreign and strange. Many couples are certainly very happy that the groom's dad is not in charge of these arrangements. Nevertheless, the essential principles found in this passage are good for us today. (The pastor-counselor will share his personal application at this point, or use the author's application points here. Space is provided in the couple's edition to write these applications.

> Possible applications from this text.
> 1. Parents who are wise know the value and importance of their children's marriage. Thus, they teach and encourage them scripturally.
> 2. The will of the Lord is earnestly sought in selecting a mate.
> 3. Scripture is never violated in determining God's will.
> 4. The heartfelt and honest prayer for the Lord's direction is critical.
> 5. Indications of the leading of the Lord are unmistakable.
> 6. The willing commitment of both parties is mandatory.
> 7. The importance of marriage can never be overstated.
> 8. The lifetime commitment to a good marriage leads to many blessings.

Continue the Session

Now that we have laid a foundation for the session today from Genesis 24, bring the counsel specifically to the couple about their marriage. When we speak of "marriage" what does that mean to the couple? It will be interesting to determine the level of maturity and understanding of the real meaning of biblical marriage. Be careful to note the correct statements and cautious in reviewing faulty statements.

Several Biblical Principles

It will be essential to invest time carefully reviewing several scriptural principles relating to the state of marriage. After reviewing these verses and statements, a clear definition of marriage should be established in the minds of the couple.

It is God's idea
"It is not good that the man should be alone; I will make him an help meet (suitable) for him…Made he a woman, and brought her unto the man…Therefore shall a man leave his father and his mother, and shall cleave unto his wife: and they shall be one flesh. And

they were both naked, the man and his wife, and were not ashamed" (Genesis 2:18-25). Marriage is God's idea and design.

It is honorable
"Marriage is honorable in all and the bed undefiled" (Hebrews 13:4a). The word for "honourable" is *timios* (TIM-ee-os) which means, "That which is precious, of great price or held in high esteem." That which is honourable or precious within marriage, is still forbidden outside of marriage (13:4b).

It is between one man and one woman and is intensely intimate
"Have ye not read, that he which made them at the beginning made them male and female, and said, For this cause shall a man leave father and mother, and shall cleave to his wife: and they two shall be one flesh? Wherefore they are no more two, but one flesh" (Matthew 19:4-6a). The concept of "one flesh" is an intense connection of spiritual, emotional, physical and sexual intimacy between one man and one woman within the gift of marriage.

It is for one lifetime
"What therefore God hath joined together, let not man put asunder" (Matthew 19:6b). It is important for the couple to understand that the decision they are making and the vows they will be taking are not a contract that has clauses and loopholes. It is a lasting covenant that is for "richer or poorer, for better or worse, in sickness and in health, as long as life shall last." Divorce is not an option. This aspect of the permanence of marriage must be emphasized and can never be overstated.

It is Wonderfully illustrated by Christ and the Church
"Wives, submit yourselves unto your own husbands, as unto the Lord. For the husband is the head of the wife, even as Christ is the head of the church: and he is the saviour of the body. Therefore as the church is subject unto Christ, so let the wives be to their own husbands in every thing. Husbands, love your wives, even as Christ also loved the church, and gave himself for it: That he might sanctify and cleanse it with the washing of water by the word, That he might present it to himself a glorious church, not having spot, or wrinkle, or any such thing; but that it should be holy and without blemish. So ought men to love their wives....For this cause shall a man leave his father and mother, and shall be joined unto his wife, and they two shall be one flesh. This is a great mystery: but I speak concerning Christ and the church. Nevertheless, let every one of you in particular so love his wife even as himself; and the wife see that she reverence her husband" (Ephesians 5:22-33).

> You may wish to point out several of the comparisons between Christ and the husband as well as the church and the wife. This is a powerful and practical illustration.

It is built upon mutual respect and priority
"Submitting yourselves one to another in the fear of God" (Ephesians 5:21). This is the opposite of the "me first" mentality so evident in the world today. There are many advocates of the "I am the most important person in the world" view who demand personal happiness regardless of who is hurt and what the cost. Mutual submission is the decision of the will to purposely hold the other person before self. It is the willingness to seek their well being rather than exalting self and demanding personal rights. This does not mean to neglect your personal well-being. Rather, find great

> From Ephesians 5, four evidences of the filling of the Holy Spirit are:
>
> 1. Communicating with psalms, hymns and spiritual songs (5:19a).
>
> 2. Expressing songs in our hearts to the Lord (5:19b).
>
> 3. Giving thanks to the Father through Christ (5:20).
>
> 4. Making others the priority over self by mutual submission because of love and respect for the Lord (5:21).

fulfillment in giving the Lord first priority, your mate the second priority and yourself the third priority.

At this point in the counseling session, discuss the practical application of these principles. Marriage is God's idea and is honorable. It must be built upon mutual respect and priority. Review with the couple the following story of Mark and Mindy. Though they are fictitious, their situation happens frequently. After reading the article, use the following questions from their homework in the counseling session.

> Mark and Mindy arrived for their premarital counseling appointment with nervousness and anticipation. They were to be married in less than six months and this would potentially be one of the most important moments in their lives.
>
> Mark grew up in a home where fighting and friction became part of daily living. Neither of Mark's parents are believers and both mom and dad were demanding and self-centered. While the fighting seldom was physical, the emotional damage was severe. Mark's mother never worked outside the home. She views her husband as a failure who never measured up to her expectations. Often she would complain that they needed more money. Mark's dad became more and more withdrawn and seemed to find his fulfillment through his work. He worked more hours, came home less frequently and though they made more money, the home became more tense and unhappy. They divorced each other four years before Mark and Mindy became engaged.
>
> Everyone in Mindy's family is a believer. Her mom is a career woman. She has taught in the same elementary school since she graduated from college. Dad owns and operates his own business. Both are supportive of each other's careers. Both are very active in their local church. Mom teaches children, and dad is an usher and treasurer. Mom is a conversationalist and very much wants to talk with her husband about everything. She teases him that after spending all day with third graders, she would like to talk with an adult for a little while. Dad is a very gracious man and often compliments his wife. They love to talk with each other and are faithful in their devotions. Their home, while not perfect, is warm, loving, respectful and spiritually minded.

This is the background of Mark and Mindy. Based on this information, discuss with the couple the following questions.

1. Knowing that our values and impression of marriage are caught from watching our parents, how would you express the most likely picture Mark and Mindy have when it comes to marriage? Mark's picture? Mindy's picture?
2. What were the obvious priorities in the families of both Mark and Mindy?
3. How would you counsel Mark and Mindy concerning the right priorities to begin establishing in their marriage, based on their pictures?
4. How were respect and priority communicated in the home in which you grew up?

> At question 4, review with the couple your observations concerning respect and priority being demonstrated in their homes and backgrounds. This is an excellent time to note the similarities and differences. Help them to see these biblically.

5. What are the ways your future mate communicates respect and priority to you?
6. How do you communicate respect and priority to your future mate?

There will be times in your counseling when this section of the session will move along quickly. Often this occurs when the couple comes from well-adjusted backgrounds and both demonstrate a degree of maturity. On the other hand, do not be surprised when love, respect and priority are not the norm. Be prepared to schedule an additional counseling appointment if necessary.

Respect and priority

Respect and priority must be evidenced now and growing at the time of the wedding. Without this, the marriage will be in trouble before it begins. The couple demonstrate respect and priority by the following characteristics.

1. You are cherished by both the Lord and myself.
2. You are desired not because of what you are able to do for me; but rather because of what you personally mean to me.
3. Your ideas, input and suggestions are not taken lightly. I will give serious consideration to what you say and what you are sensing in this particular situation.
4. Your trust in me and respect for me are things that I view as being critically important. I do not demand your trust and respect; I know I must earn it. I take this so seriously that I will be extremely careful never to betray that trust and respect.
5. Our relationship is marked by my desire to consistently respect you. I will be careful how I speak to you and about you. I will guard your character and reputation.

Conclude the Session

At this point, there may be additional questions the couple wishes to discuss. If your time does not permit, you may wish to take the questions and discuss them next time. Assign the homework for session three. The couple will work on the testing entitled "The Road Already Traveled."

The test will be used in the next several counseling sessions. For the best results, the couple should work on the test separately and not compare their answers. Copies of their answers should be made and submitted in plenty of time to allow you several weeks to read, compare, interpret and plan for the next counseling session.

If the couple is not in the habit of reading the Bible and praying together, this is a great time to begin this spiritual discipline. The books of Ephesians, John or Proverbs are great places to read as a couple.

Chapter Three—Counseling Session 3

A Great Marriage— Settle for Nothing Less

We are painfully aware of the sad state of many marriages today. It is not uncommon for many couples to assume they will have a great marriage. However, it is interesting to note that many of the same couples are not sure how to achieve a great marriage. The challenge of every counselor is to present a clear understanding of what a great marriage is and what must be done to bring it to pass. Great marriages do not just happen.

Goals for this Session

1. Evaluate the maturity of the couple in their view of marriage. Do they possess a clear understanding of the characteristics of a great marriage?
2. Detect both differences and similarities in their background and home life. They will formulate a view of marriage based on their observations at home.
3. Provide a rich spiritual time of counsel with biblical directives and principles to build a great marriage.

Prepare for this Session

Sections 1-2 of the homework "The Road Already Traveled" are the sections to be reviewed and will provide the basis of the material for this counseling session. Based on the couple's answers, the counseling session will be designed and prepared to address the major issues first, followed by the issues of lesser importance. Every counseling couple will differ in their answers and will require specific and creative preparation for counseling.

Use this homework to design the counseling approach.
Preparing for the Journey of a Lifetime
Homework for Premarital Counseling Session 3
"The Road Already Traveled"

Name _____

The information you are sharing will be held in strict confidence. Your pastor/counselor greatly desires to assist you in preparing for your marriage and home by helping you to understand your background. You have been traveling a road that has brought you to the point in life where the strong points can be strengthened and weak areas identified and changed before you enter marriage.

> The biblical counselor is welcome to use the counseling format presented, or he may prefer to work up an entirely different approach to counseling. If the counselor chooses to prepare his own, please point this out to the couple so they will understand what material comes from the author and what comes from the counselor.

Testing areas #1 and #2 deal with the couples basic view of marriage and the status of their relationship with the Lord.

Please answer these questions by using a scale of 1 to 4.
    1= Very strongly disagree, as this almost never describes my situation.
    2= Mildly disagree, as this usually does not describe my situation.
    3= Mildly agree, as this sometimes describes my situation.
    4= Strongly agree, as this usually describes my situation.

1. How I view marriage as modeled before me

_____ 1. I had the privilege of a close relationship with at least one set of grandparents.

_____ 2. I had the privilege of knowing my grandparents were happily married.

_____ 3. My grandparents were role models of how a happy marriage works.

_____ 4. I would describe my parents as happily married.

_____ 5. My parents openly express their love for each other.

_____ 6. I have frequently witnessed my parents being affectionate with other.

_____ 7. My parents love the Lord and our home. Though not perfect, it is a model of what I would like my home to be.

_____ 8. I know the role of being a spiritual leader because it was consistently modeled in our home.

_____ 9. Family time in reading the Bible and praying was common in my home.

_____ 10. I remember great family times spent together as well as special times on vacation.

2. How I view my relationship with the Lord

_____ 1. I know the Lord as my personal Savior and seek to live for Him.

_____ 2. I want to know and do the will of God because it provides great priorities in my life.

_____ 3. I read the Bible on a nearly daily basis.

_____ 4. I am a member of a Bible-believing church.

_____ 5. I have a regular ministry in my church.

_____ 6. I can honestly say my future mate and I agree on the importance of living for Christ and both of us are seeking to live for Him.

_____ 7. I have witnessed my future mate reading the Bible, praying and serving in some area of Christian service in our local church.

_____ 8. I am encouraged that my future mate is consistent in praying with me on a regular basis.

_____ 9. I can honestly say my future mate and I talk regularly about spiritual matters.

_____ 10. I know my future mate is growing spiritually and is becoming a mature disciple of the Lord Jesus Christ.

Both sections are designed to provide information that will engage the counselor and the couple in a session that focuses upon their concept of marriage, home, family and personal spiritual life. Some counselors prefer to run an additional copy of the homework. Using a blue pen for the groom and a red pen for the bride, a comparison of the answers are listed on the counselor's final worksheet. Others prefer to work up their own counseling chart based on the couple's answers.

Begin the Session

It is always in order to share in the joys the couple is experiencing as they prepare for marriage. Most counselors well remember what it was like in the weeks before their own wedding. Do you remember the joy, excitement and at times apprehension as your wedding day approached?

Take time to challenge the hearts of both the groom and bride to be committed to settling for nothing less than a great marriage. Sharing this brief acrostic of a GREAT marriage is a good way to begin this session.

G= Godliness that is consistent in daily living
R= Realistic expectations of myself and my mate
E= Endurance and endearment, as divorce is never an option
A= Affirmation and affection genuinely extended
T= Truthfulness, tactfulness and tenderness expressed consistently and daily

Continue the Session

Read Proverbs 24:3-4 to the couple. *"Through wisdom is an house builded; and by understanding it is established: and by knowledge shall the chambers be filled with all precious and pleasant riches."* Wisdom is the act of seeing with discernment. Understanding conveys the idea of responding with insight. Knowledge is the wonderful state of having a teachable spirit. The goal of this part of the counseling process is for both the bride and groom to grow in wisdom, understanding and knowledge as they prepare for their wedding and future life together as husband and wife.

Today we begin the building of a great marriage. Challenge the couple to never settle for mediocrity or anything less than the very best. When it comes to things like surgery, construction, accounting and marriage, close is not good enough. These situations and many others require something far better than "pretty good" or "close enough." Marriage is so important that nothing less than great is the goal.

The couple's view of how marriage has been modeled is very important. Many of our convictions are caught from watching as well as being taught from listening. The modeled marriages, the displayed relationships and the demonstrated levels of affection all combine to form the picture of marriage in the minds of the couple.

Section 1, statements 1-3 reflect upon the multi-generational view of marriage the couple possesses. Note the numerical rankings of these statements and build upon the importance of godly grandparents. Proverbs 13:22 says, "A good man leaveth an inheritance to his children's children…"

As strange as it may seem to the couple, they actually are preparing the way for their future grandchildren. The convictions they develop and lifestyle they model before their children are, in a very real sense, laying the foundations for future generations.

Every grandparent should leave an inheritance that is far more precious than just money. Godly grandparents leave a heritage that must be treasured.

Five Important Things Every Grandparent Can Leave to the Grandchildren
1. Concerning Christ-I trusted Him fully (Acts 16:31).
2. Concerning the Bible-I treasured it dearly (Psalm 119:72, 127).
3. Concerning sin-I turned from it deliberately (Romans 6:22).
4. Concerning blessings-I thanked the Lord daily (Psalms 95, 100).
5. Concerning my children-I taught them diligently (Deuteronomy 6:7).

If their grandparents were godly, challenge them to continue the line. If their grandparents were not godly, then today (even though the thoughts of grandchildren are probably not heavy upon their minds) a great starting point must take place. Help the couple to understand the principles of Deuteronomy 6:1-7. We heed God's instruction, grow in our reverence for Him, apply His Word to our lives and teach these things to our children so they will properly teach our grandchildren.

Section 1 statements 4-7 demonstrate the perception of the couple as it relates to the marriage of their parents. Caution is to be exercised in not allowing couples to blame their parents for their own poor attitudes and actions. On the other hand, most couples have watched marriage being played out for twenty or more years. It is important for the couple to clearly understand their background.

If statement 4 receives a low mark from either of the couple, it will be important to carefully examine why they view their parents' marriage as being unhappy. If both the bride and groom marked low, neither has a good role model in their background. Create an alternate list of several key things this couple desires in their marriage that seems lacking in the marriage of their parents.

If statement 4 receives a high mark from either or both of the counselees, hold that information until you review statement 7.

Statements 5 and 6 focus on the demonstration of love communicated and affection expressed. The counseling goal for this section will reveal the couple's perception as to how love is communicated. Romans 5:8 certainly assures us that God didn't assume we know He loved us. He communicated the depths of His love in very clear and understandable ways. The sacrifice of His own Son fully and fantastically communicates love being expressed.

It will be interesting to hear the couple explain their perception of how love is expressed. If either or both come from backgrounds of little or no loving communication, this is a great opportunity to invest in helping them to develop godly and loving convictions.

Statement 7 is extremely important. Evaluate the statements of the couple by exploring things they would change and things they wish to model. Most couples have observed qualities and situations they do not want to repeat in their marriage. What are the godly characteristics they wish to model? How will these things be accomplished?

Section 1, statement 8 deals with the role of spiritual leadership. It is important that both the bride and groom understand the biblical concept of the husband being the spiritual leader. He must humbly and gently assume it. She must lovingly and joyfully accept it.

Regardless of how the statement scored, several questions must be asked. These are crucial to the marriage. First, has the groom demonstrated consistent spiritual leadership in the dating and engagement period? How? Second, has the bride demonstrated consistently that she is willing to follow his leadership? How?

Though the wife is equal to the man in worth, value and significance, God has clearly established different roles and functions. Both are to be mutually submissive in the love, concern and care of each other (Ephesians 5:21).

The role of the wife is outlined in Ephesians 5:22-24. She is to love, cherish and respect her husband as the church loves, cherishes and respects Christ. She is to encourage her husband. Wonderful opportunities for specific prayer concerning things known only to her are part of the joy of being a faithful wife. She must be sensitive to and avoid developing situations that could be potentially dangerous and harmful to her husband. A wife must ask the Lord for grace and understanding in her role of loving submission to the leadership of her husband.

If the husband is ungodly, she still must respect the role of the husband, even if she cannot respect his actions. Peter's counsel given to the wife whose husband does not listen to God's Word is still relevant for us today. *"Likewise ye wives, be in subjection to your own husbands; that, if any obey not the word, they also may without the word be won by the conversation of the wives"* (1 Peter 3:1).

The husband is to love, cherish, protect, nurture and live for his wife as Christ does for the church. This is clearly presented in Ephesians 5:25-33. A careful examination of verses 25-27 provides the standard of the consistent, godly role of spiritual leadership. This kind of husband does not demand respect; he lives in such a way that his wife will respect him and cherish him.

A spiritual leader is one who takes seriously the condition of his household. He provides well in the physical, emotional, and spiritual realms. Cherishing God's Word is a personal and practical matter for the spiritual leader. It is personal because he is reading it regularly. It is practical because he is applying it to his life consistently. A spiritual leader seeks to understand his family. He builds trust and security in his marriage and home by the way he lives and what he says. The godly spiritual leader sets the example and provides scriptural guidance for his house and family. He is not the commander of the troops. Rather, he is more like the tender shepherd and godly pastor of his home.

This is a rare moment of opportunity for the counselor. The characteristics of the wise and godly husband must be the normal standards for believers. Though they may not sound like the typical characteristics and standards of the present, yet they are still the norm. Seize the moment and instill these values as goals in the lives of the couple.

Section 1, statements 9-10 focus upon family values, shared experiences and time invested as a family. Most surveys reveal that very few couples have grown up in homes where worship and family prayer times took place regularly. It will be important for the groom to understand this is part of his role as spiritual leader.

As you explore the shared experiences of family (or lack of shared experiences) help the couple to plan wisely how this will be addressed in their marriage. Strong marriages are those in which good memories are consistently made. Good memories are made from sharing time, attention, experiences and interests together. Creative, age-appropriate family worship and prayer time provides opportunities for spiritual growth and blessings.

Section 2, statements 1-10 focus upon the spiritual condition of the couple. It will be important to read carefully the scores of their statements and compare them with each other. Is one a stronger believer than the other? This is especially important to note if the stronger is the bride. Statement 6 is the key statement in the grouping. The statement occurs in the center of the section and is key because the earlier statements build to it. The rest of the statements are outflows from it.

> Do not limit the counseling session to the material provided. Every couple will bring a unique set of challenges to be addressed as well as strengths to be refined. Some counselors may wish to schedule additional sessions with one or both individuals.

This moment provides an incredible opportunity for the counselor to share the power of Joshua 24:15 with the couple. *"...But as for me and my house, we will serve the LORD."* Communicate with the couple the absolute importance of spiritual growth. Wonderful marriages are those which are built upon Christ and the Word of God.

From these sections of the homework as well as your personal observation, you are now beginning to get a sense of the counseling ministry ahead. Share with the couple the commendable areas and be ready with Scripture to help them address areas of concern and potential conflict.

Conclude the Session

This session will conclude by the counselor taking the couple to Deuteronomy 6. The details of the children of Israel are interesting. God is going to build a strong nation through this second generation. He does this by building one strong family at a time.

Most of the children of Israel miserably failed in the wilderness. Only a handful of individuals seemed to serve as role models for godly living along the forty-year journey in the wilderness. A new generation of families was to be established. The same principles from Deuteronomy 6, which were important for them, are just as necessary today.

Five Important Principles for Them and Us Today

1. Know who God is (verse 4).
2. Love the Lord personally and totally (verse 5).
3. Apply God's Word personally in daily living (verse 6).
4. Teach God's principles diligently to their children (verse 7).
5. Prepare the way for their grandchildren's spiritual life (verses 1-2).

Before the couple leaves, ask them to work on the financial planner (found in their edition as well as chapter 14 of your edition). Assign to them the homework of discussing the questions found on the worksheet entitled "Let's Share-Great Questions and Honest Answers." Encourage the couple to make a high priority of selecting a good time to honestly share with each other and talk about these questions found in their couple's edition.

Let's Share-Great Questions and Honest Answers

1. How do you see our careers impacting our marriage in both good and possibly difficult ways?
2. What are our individual goals relating to our careers?
3. How long do we want to wait before trying to have a baby?
4. How many children would we hope to have someday?
5. What if one of us is ready to begin our family and the other is not? How will we resolve this?
6. What will some of the changes be in our home and personal lives when the Lord allows us to have a child?
7. Are we agreed as to the method of birth control we want to use? Have we worked through this sufficiently in our minds after receiving good counsel from our physician and pastor? Are we sure this method prevents pregnancy and does not terminate it?
8. What are our plans as relating to housing? Which will work best for us right now: renting or purchasing a home?
9. How large a place do we think we really need right now?
10. How much of our income should we spend on housing? If we are not sure, are we willing to discuss this with our pastor in the premarital counseling time?
11. How important is money in our relationship?
12. What are three or four material possessions we would like to acquire someday that will require savings and a significant investment?
13. How do we define financial security?
14. What should be our attitude about indebtedness?

15. How many credit cards should we have?
16. How important should it be to pay off the balance on our credit card or cards every month?
17. Should we have a joint checking account, or should we have separate accounts?
18. How much should we save each month, and how will we invest our savings?
19. Even though retirement is a long way off, how much should we invest in our retirement account? How much should we tuck away in an emergency fund?
20. What are some of the things we will enjoy doing together around the house?
21. Will we grocery shop together? If not, whose responsibility should this be?
22. Who will be responsible for cooking? Will we share this responsibility together, and if so, how?
23. What about household chores? How will we share in these?
24. How often would we enjoy eating out?
25. How important is dating after we are married?
26. How often will we go out with our friends?
27. How often will we entertain friends in our home?
28. What are some of the good things we appreciate in the home and marriage of our parents which we would like to bring into our home and marriage?
29. What are some things we would like to change and incorporate into our home and marriage?
30. What are some of the possible conflicts that might arise out of our personality differences? How will we deal with these possibilities?
31. How will we handle holidays with our families?
32. How we will handle vacations?
33. How will we work through conflicts without hurting each other?
34. What place will the Lord hold in our home and marriage?
35. How important are daily worship and prayer as individuals and as a couple?
36. What will be our local church?
37. How important will it be in our marriage for us to serve the Lord?
38. If someday a missions trip should become a possibility, would we be willing to prayerfully consider going together?
39. What does a healthy marriage look like to us?
40. What does the role of a good husband look like? What does the role of a good wife look like?
41. What do we think a healthy sexual relationship would seem to be?
42. How often do we hope to have sex in a typical week?
43. How will we handle it when one is interested in having sex and the other is not?
44. How much do we honestly understand about the difference between a man's view of sex and a woman's view of sex?
45. How will we make big decisions together?
46. What if we discover someday that we cannot have children? Would we ever be willing to consider adoption?

47. What do you really appreciate about me? What are some areas that I really need to be working on?
48. Why do you want to marry me?
49. Would we be willing to speak with our pastor and go for marriage counseling if someday we encounter a situation we cannot resolve ourselves?
50. What are several major safeguards we want to establish to make sure our marriage stays healthy and grows throughout our lifetime?

Couples should not tackle all the questions at one sitting. They must be honest. They must understand that this how their future spouse views the situation at that time. Each couple must speak freely, carefully, graciously and forthrightly.

If there are unresolved questions, they should mark the question or questions and commit to each other that they will pray about about them and if they are still unresolved, will bring these matters to the next premarital counseling session to work through with the pastor.

Chapter Four—Counseling Session 4

My View of Home and Marriage

The first months of marriage are characterized by the two words discovery and adjustment. While most couples honestly think they know each other well at the time of their wedding, it will not take long to "discover" how many things they did not know. The response to those discoveries will require "adjustment."

> To assess the homework and define the counseling agenda, some may wish to use separate sheets to take notes. Others may wish to make copies of the homework and either use initials or different color ink to list the answers of the couple.

Goals for this Session

1. Help the couple to grasp the importance of being honest with themselves and their future mate.
2. Assist the couple in learning to appreciate the opportunity of working through issues and reaching acceptable and appropriate compromises.
3. Assess the level of maturity demonstrated by the couple as they recognize potentially conflicting situations and views as well as their willingness to resolve these issues. How is their financial budget?

Designing the Counseling Session-How to Review and Interpret the Homework

The homework entitled "The Road Already Traveled" has been designed to provide the counselor ten areas to test strengths, weaknesses, and potential conflicts. The purpose of this session is to focus on sections 3 and 4 by noting the similarities, identifying the weaknesses and detecting potential conflicts. This session should be a help in beginning to resolve these potential situations. While it is not necessary to invest a lot of time on every question or statement, take special note of those areas that demonstrate weakness or a conflicting answer.

Section 3 deals with the couple's basic view of the status of their relationship with each other.

Please answer these questions by using a scale of 1 to 4.

1= Very strongly disagree, as this almost never describes my situation.
2= Mildly disagree, as this usually does not describe my situation.
3= Mildly agree, as this sometimes describes my situation.
4= Strongly agree, as this usually describes my situation.

Chapter 4   27

3. How I view things relating to my future home and marriage

_____ 1. My future mate and I have a strong relationship of trust and mutual respect.

_____ 2. My future mate and I have talked about finances and budgeting, and we are in agreement with how our finances will be handled.

_____ 3. My future mate and I have talked about the things that make a marriage strong.

_____ 4. My future mate has a good relationship with his or her parents.

_____ 5. I have a good relationship with my parents.

_____ 6. My future mate and I have talked about the relationship we wish to have with both sets of parents after we are married.

_____ 7. My future mate and I agree on tithing and regular giving to the local church.

_____ 8. My future mate and I have talked about parenting and how to raise children.

_____ 9. My future mate and I are in agreement with the number of children we would like to have.

_____ 10. My future mate and I are in agreement with how we would like to spend holidays and vacations.

Be especially sensitive in detecting conflicting responses to any of the statements. The answers will provide you with a glimpse into the level of maturity the couple manifests in understanding future marital situations. You will see how much time and energy they have invested in talking about these matters and what level of agreement they have reached in setting convictions and standards.

Begin the Session

At this point in the premarital counseling process, it is very possible that a situation or two has developed with the couple that has not been addressed or is not on the counseling schedule. Begin the session by asking the couple how they are progressing on the fifty "Let's Share-Questions." Have they encountered things they would like to include in future counseling appointments? How many of the questions have they worked through? It is possible that something so important or pressing has developed that it must be addressed immediately? Be sensitive to such a possibility.

Begin with reading Colossians 3:12-19. Many applications can be drawn from this text. Emphasis for this session should be focused upon verse 16, "Let the word of Christ dwell in you richly…" We must allow the Scriptures to be at home in our life, lodge with us in our minds and hearts, and daily influence us in consistent ways. Then we will be able to accurately view our current situation in light of God's standards as well as to address situations that must be changed.

Section 3, statement 1 focuses on the sense of trust and mutual respect. Counseling session 2 dealt with respect and priority. It will be interesting to compare the

---

It is interesting to note from Colossians 3:

-The peace of God (Vs. 15).

-The Word of God (Vs. 16a).

-The Hymns of God (Vs. 16b).

-The Name of God (Vs. 17).

Blessed is the marriage and home of every couple who consistently remembers and observes these.

Trust is built over a period of time with the following characteristics:

-Promises kept

-Affirmation extended

-Affection demonstrated

-Commitment rehearsed

-Thoughtfulness shown

-Time together shared

-Communication remembered

-Connection enjoyed (Connection is the building of the emotional bond of "You and I belong to each other for a lifetime. It is all my love all my life.")

ratings scored by the couple for section 3, statement 1 with the level of respect and trust demonstrated in this session. Note any changes for the better or worse as the relationship continues to develop for this couple. If one or both score lower, pointed counsel as to defining trust and respect as well as how to develop both will be important. If either or both score high on this first question, rehearse briefly how they arrived at this point in their relationship.

Section 3, statements 2, 7 and Section 4, statements 1-2 focus on the maturity of the couples as relating to finances. Closely related to trust and respect, financial maturity is imperative for a good and godly marriage. Integrity and reliability in financial areas do not automatically guarantee respect and trust. However, agreement in the handling of finances plays an incredible role in successful marriages. Red flags in the statements that deal with finances will cause insecurity and disrespect.

Compare the scores of Section 3, statement 2 and Section 4, statements 1-2, to design appropriate counsel. Several financial considerations include the following.

Patterns of wasteful spending. No one is perfect and everyone at one time or another has wasted a few dollars on something that is not really necessary. The focus of this section is beyond the rare or occasional waste of funds. Is there a pattern of waste? Does the majority of the paycheck fly away with little or no accounting? Does the couple even know where the paycheck has gone?

Impulsive buying or spending. Marriages have been wrecked because of the impulsive spending sprees of one or both individuals. An impulsive buyer purchases items that are not necessary or are even duplicated by other purchases and runs up credit card debt on things that will never be used, often are not needed and sometimes are not even desirable.

Out of control credit and indebtedness. At this point in the counseling session, it is important to direct the couple to the worksheet entitled, "Our Financial Planner." After discussing the previous financial principles, review their planner with them. You may assist them with typical expected expenses found in your community and surrounding area. If they need addition time, you may wish to include this section of counseling at a later session. It is very possible that the couple has not talked seriously about their financial situation, even though the wedding is approaching. This is a suggested planner. You may wish to substitute your own planner at this point if you so choose.

Our Financial Planner

Monthly Income

Gross Monthly Income _____

Investment Income _____

Total Monthly Income _____

Monthly Deductions

    Tithe and Offering   _____

    Federal Income Tax   _____

    State/Local Taxes   _____

    Social Security/Medicare   _____

    Total Monthly Gross Income   _____

    Total Monthly Tithe/ Taxes   _____

        Total Remaining Usable Monthly Income _____

Expenses: Housing Costs

    Mortgage/ Rent   _____

    Homeowners/ Renters Insurance   _____

    Property Taxes   _____

    Repairs/Improvements   _____

    Utilities:

    Electricity   _____   Gas   _____

    Water/Sewer   _____   Telephone   _____

        Total Housing Expenses _____

Expenses: Food and Grocery .... _____

Expenses: Heath Insurance, Medical Expenses .... _____

Expenses: Transportation

    Car payment   _____

    Insurance   _____

    Gas/oil/repairs   _____

    Miscellaneous tolls/parking   _____

        Total Transportation _____

Expenses: Credit Cards/Loans .... _____

Expenses: Entertainment / Recreation / Personal .... _____

Savings/ Investments .... _____

        Total Monthly Usable Income _____

        Total Monthly Projected Expenses _____

        Current Status (Positive or Negative) _____

Mature individuals are timely in paying their bills and assuming responsibility for their finances. Does the couple have a godly view of stewardship? Do they honor the Lord in their finances (Proverbs 3:9-10)? Certainly the Lord is glorified (1 Corinthians 10:31) by maintaining a good credit score with timely payments and financial integrity. This is a wonderful opportunity to help the couple in the area of their tithe, offerings, and generosity with the Lord.

Section 3, statements 3-10 focus on the marks of a strong marriage. While it may sound humorous to encourage the couple to think of a waffle (another acrostic), the purpose is two-fold. First, by using a word picture with an acrostic, the principles are often more easily learned and remembered. Secondly, these six principles, though not exhaustive, if practiced consistently will be key building blocks in the growth of a healthy and strong marriage. The word to remember is "Waffle!"

W= Wholly follow the Lord. Peter. admonishes believers to remember "…Christ also suffered for us, leaving us an example, that ye should follow his steps" (1 Peter 2:21). Strong is the marriage when both husband and wife truly and wholly follow the Lord.

A= Appreciation, affirmation, and affection are daily and consistently present in the marriage. Over time, two kinds of marriages will develop. The first is marked by taking each other and their marriage for granted. While it is not necessarily a deliberate decision, it is nevertheless a serious deterioration of a healthy and vibrant relationship. This marriage slowly loses the sense of how extremely precious the mate is and how much the mate means. It is a slow drifting apart from the closeness the Lord intends for married couples.

In the second kind of marriage, the couple grows closer and genuinely cherishes each other. This couple treats each other in such a way as to express appreciation, affirmation, and affection. Keeping the marriage fresh and healthy requires regular attention and devotion.

F= Forgiveness is sought and granted. Never will two individuals, from two different backgrounds and with two interesting personalities, live together in total and complete harmony without an occasional misunderstanding or disagreement. Paul writes to the Ephesian believers and reminds them of the joy of forgiving others, as God, for the sake of Christ, has forgiven them (Ephesians 4:32).

Forgiveness is the cancellation of the indebtedness that comes from offending or wounding another. Forgiveness sought is the action of the offender who is truly sorry for the offense. Some offenders ignore their actions and assume it is a little thing. However, those little things can accumulate and become heavy, weighty matters. Large buildings crumble under the weight of heavy snow, which accumulates one tiny flake at a time.

When repentance takes place on the part of the offender and restoration is sought, genuine forgiveness cancels the debt and sets in motion the steps toward restoration. Genuine forgiveness does not bring up the offense again or use it against the other. The forgiveness of the Father for the sake of Christ is always the basis of our forgiveness of others.

> The counselor will be wise to remind the couple of the trigger words that only deepen the fracture caused by an offense. The two trigger words are "always" and "never." You always… You never…
>
> Proverbs 25:11 reminds us, "A word fitly spoken is like apples of gold in pictures of silver." The hurling of a trigger word is far from apples of gold!

> A note of caution concerning forgiveness must be noted as pertaining to cases of abuse and endangerment. This is the exception to the forgiveness rule. While forgiveness may be granted, if there is the potential for harm, physical restoration may be impossible.
>
> Exercise extreme caution and wisdom in dealing with abusive situations. Issues of anger and abuse demand a halt to proceeding with wedding plans. Intense counseling beyond the typical premarital and plenty of time will be needed to insure that change has truly taken place.

F= Fellowship, the sharing together of that which we have in common with each other and the Lord. John describes this wonderful fellowship as being both vertical (between the believer and the Lord) as well as horizontal (extended from believer to believer) in 1 John 1:3-7. Malachi reminds the Old Testament saints of the companionship aspect in marriage (Malachi 2:14). While it is not uncommon for everyone to need a little space and personal time, healthy marriages thrive from shared experiences and the development of common interests through fellowship.

L= Love expressed consistently. Some chuckle at the joke about the man who said, "When we were married, the preacher asked me if I would love and cherish her? I said I do. If anything changed I would let her know. Thirty-three years later nothing has changed; so I assume she knows I still love her." While this may cause a smile to some, it surely does not bring a smile to the wife who has not heard her husband share his love for her for the last thirty-three years.

Genuine love must be expressed as God does (John 3:16) and demonstrated as only the Lord could (Romans 5:8). If the couple genuinely walks with the Lord, expressions and demonstrations of love will be deliberate, consistent and creative.

E= Example of trust and devotion. Remember that little things can cause great destruction. James illustrates this truth relating to the tongue and the way we use it (James 3:3-5). A small match carelessly discarded can cause great destruction in a dry forest. Likewise, the key ingredients of trust and devotion are not usually destroyed by one single act of sabotage; frequently they are eroded by the accumulation of little thoughtless acts of selfishness, insensitivity and rudeness.

"Waffle" may sound like a humorous thing to share; but surely these are the essential ingredients necessary for a healthy marriage.

Section 4 deals with current situations.

Please answer these questions by using a scale of 1 to 4.

1= Very strongly disagree, as this almost never describes my situation.
2= Mildly disagree, as this usually does not describe my situation.
3= Mildly agree, as this sometimes describes my situation.
4= Strongly agree, as this usually describes my situation.

4. My current situation

_____ 1. Financially, I live within my means and adhere to a budget.

_____ 2. Financially, my future mate lives within his/her means and adheres to a budget.

_____ 3. My future mate and I have a good level of communication and I am satisfied with it.

_____ 4. I feel like I can talk with my future mate about anything and will have his/her attention and understanding.

A useful and practical outline on the tongue includes:

The tongue of the just is as choice silver (Proverbs 10:20).

The tongue of the wise uses knowledge aright (Proverbs 15:2).

The tongue of the learned knows how to speak a word in season to him that is weary (Isaiah 50:4).

_____ 5. My future mate and I are currently serving the Lord in some capacity.

Finances, communication, and service are critically important. Each couple will present a unique set of challenges and needs in creative planning for maximum counseling effectiveness. Depending on the situations uncovered by the homework as well in the counseling session, it may be necessary to schedule an additional meeting.

Section 4, statements 3-4 focus upon the level of communication demonstrated by the couple. Section 4 statements 3 and 4 are very interesting. It is not uncommon for the man to be satisfied with the level of their communication, while the lady is dissatisfied. Many men are startled when their future mate scores a low number on the level of satisfaction for communication.

It will be important for the couple to begin to establish good communication skills now in their relationship. Are their parents good role models in communication? How does the future bride speak to her father? How does the future groom speak to his mother? The way the couple speaks to their parents often provides glimpses into the future level of respect and communication in marriage.

Words can easily become deadly bullets fired carelessly toward the marriage partner. These word bullets are tones of sarcasm, ridicule, needless accusations, negative comparisons with others, hurtful put-downs, negative facial gestures and hateful words. James was right. The use of the tongue and our words can cause great damage (James 3:1-10).

The opposite is also true. Relationships, friendships and marriages are greatly encouraged and nurtured by the appropriate use of godly words. King David said, "I will take heed to my ways, that I sin not with my tongue…" (Psalm 39:1). "A wholesome tongue is a tree of life" (Proverbs 15:4). Wise couples learn early the importance of good communication. Listen with an open mind. Look at the partner speaking. Refrain from interrupting. Think about what the partner has said. Even if one disagrees, respect and thoughtfulness must be shown.

Share with the couple your observations of their communication during the counseling process. Ephesians 4:15 reminds us to be "Speaking the truth in love…" so that maturity can take place. It may not be easy to confront weak areas of communication. However, it is much better to address these areas now rather than later in marriage.

Statement 5 deals with the importance of the local church and service. This is a good opportunity for you to help the couple establish strong convictions about their ministry and the blessings of serving.

Conclude the Session

This has been a time of making a major investment in the home and marriage of this couple. The counselor has added counseling strategies and biblical principles to meet the needs of the couple. Homework will be given that will uniquely fit the counseling needs of the couple as perceived by you, the counselor. In addition, the homework entitled "The Journey of Ron and Lisa" will be assigned along with the accompanying questions to be completed in the couple's edition before the next session. A word of explanation regarding the homework will be in order. Ron and Lisa, though fictitious, demonstrate the need to be honest and real with self, others, and the Lord. This will be discussed in the next session.

Encourage the couple by reminding them that, even if several changes are needed, the Lord specializes in changing, restoring and building up that which is in need. Emphasize the importance of heeding God's Word and building their lives on Christ right now (Matthew 7:24-29).

You may wish to supplement additional counseling notes and Biblical principles throughout this session. Be alert for any attitude of indifference on the part of either the bride or groom as relating to the importance of resolving potential conflicts. Occasionally one of the partners may still have the attitude of waiting until after the marriage to make adjustments. Now is much better than later!

Chapter Five—Counseling Session 5

Making a Marriage That Works and Grows

As the counseling sessions progress, it should become increasingly clear as to whether or not this couple is ready for marriage. Session 5 measures several areas relating to marriage. Use the story of Ron and Lisa as well as the questions relating to them for the starting point as well as additional areas of counsel to be addressed. The answers in sections 5-9 of the "Road Already Traveled" will provide the basis for the remainder of this counseling session.

Goals for this Session

The homework should assist you in evaluating several situations both individually as well as in their relationship as a couple.

1. Assess the spiritual condition of the couple.
2. Be mindful of the couple's level of maturity.
3. Compare the background of the couple for differences and similarities.
4. Continue to assist the couple with their communication skills.
5. Note the similarities and differences between the personalities of the individuals. How will these affect their future marriage?
6. Assess the couple's preparedness for marriage. Do you detect problems such as anger issues, unresolved conflicts, financial difficulties or deficiencies in their view of marriage?

Prepare for this Session

This session will require creativity and significant preparation time. Major issues will be addressed in this session that will require scriptural direction as well as wisdom from the Lord. The following is a possible counseling agenda for conducting this session.

Counseling Agenda for (Bride's name) and (Groom's name)

1. Opening prayer.
2. Read the story of Ron and Lisa and review their homework.
    A. Review bride's answers to questions 1-4
    B. Review groom's answers to questions 1-4
    C. Review bride's answers to question 5
    D. Review groom's answers to question 5

Chapter 5 35

3. Key principles to work through in this part of the session:
   A. An honest and accurate perception of self
   B. An honest and accurate perception of mate
   C. Every person has strong areas on which to build. We will look specifically at several of these. Note how often one individual's strengths will complement the future mate's weak areas.
   D. Every person has weak areas to refine. We will also note several of these that may potentially result in conflict.
4. Review and compare the answers for sections 6-7. How do they describe themselves? How does your mate describe each other?
5. Review and compare the answers for sections 8-9. What are the similarities? What are the differences? How will these be reflected in typical marriage situations? How can we biblically resolve potential or actual conflicts?

This is a brief outline for a projected counseling agenda. As you read and interpret the homework answers, noting the complementary situations as well as the potentially conflicting situations, you will need to write out the counseling model unique to this couple.

The remainder of this chapter is devoted to assisting you with this session's agenda. The homework, "The Journey of Ron and Lisa" is presented. Homework answers and the application of the counseling materials are also covered. As you study through the material, make additional notes with biblical principles in the right margin.

Homework for Pre-Marital Counseling Session 5
The Journey of Ron and Lisa—"Getting to Know the Real Me"

> Ron and Lisa have been married for thirteen years. Though they grew up in the same general area in the rural farming lands of Iowa, their backgrounds are very different. As you read the story of their marriage journey, think through the importance of understanding your mate as well as yourself.
>
> Ron's family were hard-working farmers who seldom took time off as they worked from before dawn until late in the day, almost every day. Ron's mom and dad were young children when their individual families both moved to Iowa to work the land. Five brothers and three sisters caused Ron's life to be filled with noise, laughter, and times of rivalry that caused mom to swat the children with a rolled up towel! "Out of my kitchen and stop that racket!" often were the words mom shouted in good nature and with a smile on her face as she scooted the children on their way.
>
> The Lord was the center of the life of Ron's family. Though the farm required many hours every day, the Lord was honored early in the morning. Individually each member of the family had quiet moments in the Word of God and prayer. Breakfast took place together after dad had already worked several hours. No food was served until dad carefully took the old family Bible off the shelf in the kitchen and brought it to

the table. The atmosphere was not harsh or rigid. However, each child knew this was not the time to wiggle or giggle. Dad read a portion of the Word and one of the children would be asked to lead in prayer and thank the Lord for the day and the food. As soon as the "Amen" was spoken, all quietness and serenity were shattered as massive amounts of food were passed and most of the family talked at the same time.

Immediately after supper, as soon as the dishes were taken to the sink, the family gathered in the living room of the old farm house for what was called "evening worship." Ron's mom often played a hymn or two on the old upright piano. Even though it was not in tune and even though the family was not composed of great singers, wonderful times of music and worship took place around that old piano. Dad would often read from the Bible and then make up a story of his own that would illustrate what the family just read.

The children grew older and one by one left the home for college or marriage. The family circle grew smaller. Ron, who was number six in the line of nine children, was old enough to remember the great evenings of large family gatherings in that small living room. Even better were the times when guests were present and everything stopped for "evening worship." By the time Ron was preparing for marriage, the family gatherings were less than half the size; but they were precious still in the learning of God's ways and growing as a family of believers.

Ron had a personality that was very outgoing. He loved to meet people and conversation came easily for him. As Ron would be sent into town on an errand, dad would often remind him, "Ronnie, get back here with the tractor part as soon as you can. Don't stop and talk with everyone you meet." Ron would laugh and wave to his dad as he jumped into his rusty pickup that had over 314,000 miles on it. Dust from the driveway flew as Ron headed to town eagerly waiting who he might see at the parts supply store.

Everyone seemed to love Ron's sense of humor and generosity. He was funny; but still had a concern for others that was demonstrated by his impulsive willingness to share. Sometimes Ron gave away most of his paycheck because someone else had a need. Later, there would be a time or two when he would have trouble paying a bill because with little or no thought of his own needs, he gave away a large part of his paycheck.

Enthusiasm was second nature to Ron. Nothing daunted him. He awoke long before the alarm would go off. Eager and excited about the day, Ron often annoyed the two other brothers who shared the room but did not share the same outlook. By the time the alarm would sound, Ron had already thought of two jokes, ten questions and fifteen things to talk about. The other two brothers were simply trying to remember where they were and what day it was! Pillows often flew at Ron as the other brothers covered their heads with their blankets.

Ron had a hard time understanding why others were not as cheerful and excited about life. Lisa had noticed Ron on several occasions. He was always talking with someone and frequently would end the conversation with laughter and a gentle slap on the shoulder of the other men as he left the group. She would not be noticed by Ron until Lisa's family visited the church where Ron and his family attended. Right in the middle of the hymn Ron glanced in Lisa's direction and spotted her. There, right before his eyes, was the most beautiful young woman he had ever seen. Ron didn't get very much out of the service that Sunday. Though Ron had often been accused of exaggerating, this time he really meant it when he whispered to himself, "She is the most incredibly beautiful woman I have ever seen." The service could not end fast enough for Ron that Sunday. Several were surprised that Ron didn't speak in return to them as he flew past six pews of worshippers to meet the beautiful, but very shy and introverted, Lisa.

She spotted him coming. It would be no exaggeration to say she could feel her face starting to burn as she knew it was turning red. Oh, to stop that blushing! "Why does it always come at the worst time in the world?" she thought. Ron introduced himself and began to talk non-stop. His normal extroverted personality seemed in overdrive as he talked with the visitor named Lisa.

Lisa's family lived in the neighboring town about twenty miles from Ron and his family. Hard work was a normal part of their lives but farming was not the family business. Lisa's dad was a professor in a local community college and her mother taught in the elementary school in town. Lisa was the oldest of the sibling group of three daughters. She and her family were close and enjoyed doing things together.

Lisa's personality was very quiet, calm, and easygoing. Often she heard her parents talk about the need to find a church somewhere, sometime. She never pressed the issue, assuming that sooner or later they would get around to it. Studies came fairly easy to Lisa. That was a huge blessing, because Lisa often would procrastinate in many areas, including her school work. Even though mom and dad were in public education, Lisa had the attitude of "When it comes to term papers, why start today what could be put off until tomorrow?"

There were times of tension in the family between her parents and Lisa as mom and dad did not share this same viewpoint. Though she was a procrastinator, Lisa was very dependable. She was never early in completing an assignment; but she was consistently on time. She was totally dependable in other areas as well. Seldom did Lisa miss an obligation or fail to keep a promise.

Without a doubt, the most difficult thing in the world for Lisa was to make decisions. One of the reasons she would procrastinate on her term papers was found in trying to decide the subject for her writing. This difficulty in making decisions translated into most areas of her life. Many times her sisters would become impatient with her as they waited for her to decide which sweater to wear or what color slacks to select. Several times she was left behind because she was having trouble making up her mind again.

Lisa's family had very little interest in spiritual things. That started to change when a good friend died suddenly as the result of a tragic automobile accident. Lisa's family was deeply moved at the funeral service conducted by Pastor Winters. They were impressed by his gentle and loving remarks. His message directly from the Bible was amazing and something brand new to them. However, it was the loving and caring congregation of the church who reached out to the family of the deceased friend that convinced Lisa's family that something big was missing in their lives. Whatever this congregation had, Lisa's family needed.

Two weeks later, during an appointment Lisa's dad made with Pastor Winters, Lisa's family together placed their faith in Christ. Pastor Winter's could not remember the last time he led an entire family to the Lord. Lisa's family would visit Pastor Winters's church the next Sunday.

True to form, while everyone else was very nervous about this new activity for Sunday morning, Lisa was even-keeled and collected. The hardest part of the entire morning for her was to decide between her yellow dress and the pink outfit which was given to her for her last birthday. The rest of the family was heading for the car when she finally decided on the yellow outfit. Dad had to drive hurriedly to keep from being late. Lisa noticed Ron that first Sunday but was too shy to hardly look up when he and a group of friends walked nearby.

It was on the second visit that Ron had discovered her. Soon they began dating and truly enjoyed getting to know each other. Lisa found Ron amusing, funny, and animated, never running out of good stories or sharing news of things that were going on in his life. Lisa was so easy to date. She seldom had a preference as to where they would eat a bite of lunch together. Ron did notice that she seemed to have a hard time deciding even on little things on the menu. She was a good and calming influence in his life, and he encouraged her to be a little more outgoing. A year later they were engaged, and six months later they married.

Now thirteen years and two children ages 9 and 6 later, Ron and Lisa are making an appointment for marriage counseling. Pastor Winters has retired; but their current Pastor has scheduled an intake session to gather information and data about Ron and Lisa.

Ron has told the pastor, "I love my wife, but she never gets around to anything. She has unfinished projects all over the house. I don't think she even loves me anymore. She never is affectionate. She is unresponsive to me in every way. And stubborn- I want to tell you pastor, is she ever stubborn!"

> Through her tears, Lisa said, "Pastor, I can see why my husband feels this way. But he has pushed me away. He makes promises he does not keep. He has forgotten both my birthday and our anniversary. He talks; but never stops to listen. In fact, he is always talking, talking, talking; but never listening. We are behind in our bills because Ron has insisted on helping his sister and her family. I am sorry they are out of work; but we have bills too. When I tried to tell him how concerned about this I was, he made a joke about it and gave them additional funds. I really don't think my husband loves us. He is always running here and there to help everyone else."

As the bridal couple, imagine you are the counseling pastor.

1. What are several key characteristics of Ron's personality?
2. What are several key characteristics of Lisa's personality?
3. What are several key areas in which the two different personalities complement each other?
4. What are several key areas in which the two different personalities clash?
5. What are several key characteristics of your personality?
6. What are several key characteristics of your future mate's personality?
7. What are several ways your personalities complement each other? What are several ways your personalities clash?

After briefly introducing the subject of conflicts because of the differences in personalities in the fictional lives of Ron and Lisa, a good foundation is laid to begin discussing the differences in the lives of the counselees.

What a privilege it is to design a custom-made approach to premarital counseling in this session! Each counselor will employ his own agenda for biblically addressing the situations that will surface through interpreting the homework. As you design the counseling agenda for this session, invest time and prayer in listing the similarities and differences. Determine how many sessions will be required to address the areas of concern that surfaced.

Sections 5-8 provide a snapshot of the spiritual condition of the couple.

In this section, simply check the statements that best describe you.

5. My Walk with the Lord

_____ I know the Lord as Savior

_____ I sometimes doubt my salvation

_____ I struggle with the assurance of salvation

_____ I am growing in my spiritual life

_____ I read the Bible nearly daily

_____ I pray throughout the day

_____ I am assured my future mate knows the Lord as personal Savior.

_____ I grew up in a Christian home

_____ I am the first Christian in my family

_____ My future mate and I pray regularly together

_____ My future mate and I agree on the church in which we will be members

_____ My mate and I agree on how frequently we will attend our local church.

_____ My mate and I enjoy serving in our local church

_____ The Lord has first priority in my life

Section 5 focuses on the spiritual condition of the couple. Wise counselors seek to discern if both the bride and groom genuinely know Christ as Savior. Next, a great opportunity presents itself for the counselor to help the couple begin their marriage with good and godly convictions concerning the priority of Christ and the local church.

As you review the worksheet, what are the areas that are strong and commendable? What are the areas of concern that must be addressed in counseling? Deuteronomy 6 and Joshua 24:15 provide wonderful biblical principles to share.

6. Which of the following statements best describe you?

_____	Outgoing, friendly	_____	Humorous, funny
_____	Enjoys meeting people	_____	Talkative
_____	Enthusiastic	_____	Generous
_____	Undisciplined	_____	Disorganized
_____	Exaggerates at times	_____	Can be insensitive
_____	Cold, unsympathetic	_____	Hostile, angry
_____	Unforgiving	_____	Domineering
_____	Opinionated	_____	Proud
_____	Productive	_____	Practical, logical
_____	Self-confident	_____	Calm, quiet
_____	Easy going	_____	Diplomatic
_____	Dependable	_____	Reluctant leader
_____	Unmotivated	_____	Stubborn

_____ Indecisive   _____ Fearful

_____ Analytical   _____ Perfectionist

_____ Sensitive   _____ Self sacrificing

_____ Moody   _____ Critical

_____ Revengeful   _____ Very loving

7. Which of the following statements best describe your future mate?

_____ Outgoing, friendly   _____ Humorous, funny

_____ Enjoys meeting people _____ Talkative

_____ Enthusiastic   _____ Generous

_____ Undisciplined   _____ Disorganized

_____ Exaggerates at times _____ Can be insensitive

_____ Cold, unsympathetic   _____ Hostile, angry

_____ Unforgiving   _____ Domineering

_____ Opinionated   _____ Proud

_____ Productive   _____ Practical, logical

_____ Self-confident   _____ Calm, quiet

_____ Easy going   _____ Diplomatic

_____ Dependable   _____ Reluctant leader

_____ Unmotivated   _____ Stubborn

_____ Indecisive   _____ Fearful

_____ Analytical   _____ Perfectionist

_____ Sensitive   _____ Self-sacrificing

_____ Moody   _____ Critical

_____ Revengeful   _____ Very loving

Sections 6 and 7 provide the counselor the opportunity to evaluate how the couple perceive both themselves and their future mate. Be alert for inaccurate perceptions as well as unrealistic expectations in this section of the testing. Note the similarities of personality as well as differences. Patterns of behavior as well attitudes will be revealed in this section.

Remember that the purpose of this section of testing will assist you in evaluating the following three areas:

1. How similar is the couple? Are these similarities helpful or do they present potential conflicts or weak areas?
2. How different is the couple? Are these the types of differences that will complement each other? Are these differences potentially problem areas?
3. How accurate is the couple's evaluation of each other? This is important in that the level of maturity will be measured at this point.

8. Select the following statements that best describe the home in which you grew up.

_____	I was an only child	_____	Godly father
_____	Godly mother	_____	Spiritually-minded home
_____	Warm, loving	_____	Love was demonstrated
_____	Fun, laughter	_____	Generally happy home
_____	People visited often	_____	Devotions together
_____	Cold, unloving	_____	Harsh, demanding
_____	Perfectionist demands	_____	Spontaneous
_____	Quiet, lonely at times	_____	Often noisy, activities
_____	Organized, orderly	_____	Well-disciplined
_____	Too permissive	_____	Too disciplined
_____	Favoritism shown	_____	Good parenting
_____	Regular vacations	_____	All shared chores
_____	Talked together	_____	Ignored problems
_____	Resolved problems	_____	Generous
_____	Often had at least one meal together daily		
_____	Respect shown	_____	Respect taught consistently

9. Select the following statements that best describe the home in which your mate grew up.

_____	I was an only child	_____	Godly father
_____	Godly mother	_____	Spiritually-minded home
_____	Warm, loving	_____	Love was demonstrated

_____	Fun, laugher	_____	Generally happy home
_____	People visited often	_____	Devotions together
_____	Cold, unloving	_____	Harsh, demanding
_____	Perfectionist demands	_____	Spontaneous
_____	Quiet, lonely at times	_____	Often noisy, activities
_____	Organized, orderly	_____	Well-disciplined
_____	Too permissive	_____	Too disciplined
_____	Favoritism shown	_____	Good parenting
_____	Regular vacations	_____	All shared chores
_____	Talked together	_____	Ignored problems
_____	Resolved problems	_____	Generous
_____	Often had at least one meal together daily		
_____	Respect shown	_____	Respect taught consistently

Sections 8 and 9 provide one more significant opportunity for the couple to seriously consider the background and home life from which they have traveled. How couples view marriage often is based on what they have observed in their home and family.

Be alert to key considerations in the evaluation of home and family.

1. Was the home spiritually minded?
2. Were either set of parents perfectionists with standards hard or impossible to achieve?
3. How were problems handled?
4. What was the typical level of communication within the home and marriage?
5. Was the home organized and orderly or disorganized and chaotic?
6. What is to be noted of the typical discipline in the home?

Begin the Session

Welcome the couple and assure them that you appreciate the opportunity to work in the private areas of their lives. Many couples might think of this session as getting to know the real self. Some counselors may wish to share an illustration or two from their own marriage that required adjustment. (These should not be overly intimate and always with the permission of your wife.) It might be helpful to the couple to understand some of the similarities of your backgrounds as well as a few differences.

Using the test questions from "The Journey of Ron and Lisa" as well as the evaluation of sections 5-9, develop the session with the help of the proposed outline at the beginning of the chapter.

This is an important time for the couple to know the similarities and differences they are going to face. By this time in their engagement, couples typically have already discovered some of these areas. Many situations have never been addressed, and unfortunately, some couples just assume they will wait until after their marriage and somehow then, they will change their mate. At this point it is essential to consider several key principles. Depending on the outcome of the homework, additional counseling appointments may be needed to adequately address the issues.

Key Principles to Accept and Remember

Every couple who comes for premarital counseling will present a different set of strengths, weaknesses, convictions and goals. No two couples will be identical. However, there are several key principles every couple will need to consider and upon which they must act.

Every couple comes from a different background

No two couples have experienced an identical background. Some may have a strong Christian background, while others come from an unchurched, unsaved background. Some may have experienced a happy childhood while others endured a very difficult and unhappy home life. It is important to understand the roads the couples have traveled to get to this moment of life.

Every couple must take an honest inventory of their past, present and future goals

King David was very honest in his prayer. "Search me, O God, and know my heart: try me, and know my thoughts: And see if there be any wicked way in me, and lead me in the way everlasting" (Psalm 139:23-24). Most couples will be apprehensive in being honest about self. However, for the very best foundation to be laid for marriage, honest evaluation is very important.

Every couple has strong areas to build upon and weak areas to refine

As the counselor evaluates the homework entitled, "The Road Already Traveled" you will see areas that reflect similarities and differences as well as strengths and weaknesses. The counseling appointment today is pointed because you will address critical situations and issues. It is much wiser to address them now and resolve them before the marriage rather than risk their surfacing as a major problem after the wedding.

In an earlier session, you read Proverbs 24:3-4 to the couple. Remind them of these verses once again. "Through wisdom is an house builded; and by understanding it is established. And by knowledge shall the chambers be filled with all precious and pleasant riches." Wisdom is the act of seeing with discernment. Understanding gives the idea of responding with insight. Knowledge is the wonderful state of having a teachable spirit. The goal of this part of the counseling process is that both the bride and groom will have that wisdom, understanding and knowledge in preparing for the building of their home.

Depending on the severity of the weak or conflicting areas, continue the process of counseling in addressing several of these. The length of this counseling session will depend upon how close to the date of the wedding this session takes place and how many issues the couple has presented in their homework. You may need to schedule an additional counseling session depending on the number of conflicts.

The flexibility and creativity of the biblical counselor will be demonstrated more in this counseling session than any other. As you prepare for this counseling session, much time will be invested in comparing answers, strengths and weaknesses.

Biblically resolving conflicts

Regardless of the weak or conflicting situation to be addressed, several key principles must be established in resolving these matters. The Biblical prescription for resolving conflicting matters is detailed in Ephesians 4.

1. Always attack the problem, never attack each other (4:15).
2. Identify the situation and call it what it really is-sin (4:22). Do not blame it on your parents. Do not blame others for the problem. Be willing to identify the works of the old nature and acknowledge that they are sin.
3. Ask the Lord to help you view the situation from a biblical perspective (4:23-24).
4. Be totally honest about your role in this matter (4:25). Do not be deceptive.
5. Do not become defensive and "clam up" refusing to talk or speak about the conflict (4:26).
6. Ask the Lord to give you grace and to restrain your anger so you won't say things you will later regret (4:27).
7. Be willing to ask the Lord to make big changes in your personal life (4:28-32).

Conclude the Session

Reassure the future groom and bride that every couple before them and every couple after them will have their areas of strengths and weaknesses. You may wish to make the next appointment with them at this time. If additional appointments are needed to work through these issues, the appointment should be scheduled to see the couple as soon as convenient. If no additional appointments are necessary, homework may be designed and assigned that you want them to do. The next appointment will focus on keys to connection and the joy of intimacy in the marriage relationship.

Chapter Six—Counseling Session 6

The Goal and Joy of Intimacy

The date for the wedding is drawing closer. Another home and family will be taking its place among the many thousands of homes and families. When viewing the couple and knowing the wedding is approaching, many pastors cannot help but wonder what it really will be like in the marriage over which they are to officiate. Will the couple be another sad statistic of failure? Or, will they have a lovingly-connected, close and intimate marriage? How do I speak to them about the most private nature of the premarital counseling sessions-their sexuality? This session is designed to help the couple prepare for connection and intimacy.

Goals for this Session

1. Help the couple to arrive at a clear picture of biblical intimacy.
2. Identify with the couple those things which certainly will damage intimacy. The destructors of intimacy are both active and inactive. There are specific things individuals do either intentionally or unintentionally that destroy closeness. These actions are identified as actively destructive. Inactive destructors are those which are characterized by carelessness, thoughtlessness and selfishness. Though not active in specific ways, these passive, "left-to-themselves" matters of inattentiveness to the mate will destroy the joy of closeness found in marital intimacy. Addressing them now in this session will help the couple and keep the pastor-counselor from much work later.
3. Helping the couple to develop a healthy biblical view of God's gift of sexuality will be an extremely important goal in this session.
4. Allowing the couple to bring to the counseling session any questions or matters not covered.
5. Helping the couple understand the difference between intimacy and sexual relationship explains the closeness of emotional bonding. Sexual activity is an expression of intimacy; but is not exclusive to intimacy.
6. A decision on your part as the pastor-counselor as to whether or not you will marry this couple must be determined no later than this session. As you have worked through five intensely personal sessions with this couple, by now you have a good idea as to how the Lord would have you proceed. No couple is 100% ready for marriage. There are many adjustments ahead for every couple. However, does this couple manifest the qualities spiritually, emotionally, financially and even in maturity, for you to proceed? You must give the couple an answer. This session typically is the deadline for that answer.

> It is wise to prepare a written statement as to guidelines for weddings. I found it helpful to have the endorsement of the board of deacons standing with me in this policy. Some churches incorporate such guidelines in the policy section of the constitution

Begin the Session

Assure the couple of your love for them and how much you have been praying for them. Briefly review the purpose of the session today and how very important this is to the Lord as well as to them personally. Assure the couple it is not your intention to unnecessarily embarrass them; explain that every couple you marry walks through this information together.

Following your prayer time, ask one of the bridal couple to read 1 Timothy 3:1-7. Both the groom and bride may be somewhat surprised that they are reading about the marriage, home and family qualifications of their pastor. Ideally, nothing in the pastor's marriage should be exclusive to him and not others. Neither marriage will be perfect. For sure, neither home will raise perfect children. As for the development of a close and intimate relationship, neither marriage will be effortless and automatic. The same qualifications for the marriage and family life of the pastor should be the same goals and standards for the home and marriage of every believer.

Emphasize the phrase found in 1 Timothy 3:2 that states, "…The husband of one wife…." The couple must understand that your role as the husband-pastor is not simply to make it through a lifetime without getting a divorce. Rather, your marriage demands the proper investment and the goal of producing a husband who is a "one-woman" kind of man. The beauty of this goal reaches far beyond the parsonage!

What a joy it is to look the future groom in the eyes and tell him, "My prayer and goal for you is that you would determine in your heart every day to be a one-woman kind of man." Likewise, as you look at the future bride, share with her, "It is my prayer and goal for you that as you want your future husband to be a one-woman kind of man, you also will become a one-man kind of woman." Though many people will touch your lives daily, the intimate fellowship of a husband and wife is that which must never be shared with another as long as life lasts.

God, the creator and designer of marriage, greatly desires this couple to experience the joy and preciousness of intimacy. Some marriages that stay together for a life time never achieve or experience this open, vital, fresh and growing state of becoming a one partner kind of person.

What in the World is this Intimacy of which We Speak?

The primary picture of intimacy is that bonding and closeness known as connection in the relationship. There is a sense in connection intimacy of being familiar, personal, or private with another person. A commitment is made and consistently reinforced that our connection is of great value and that which is to be cherished. Thus, it must not be violated nor shared.

Intimacy is that unique and amazing level of connection shared by one husband and one wife for lifetime. Biblical intimacy holds back nothing helpful or blessed from my marriage partner. It makes me vulnerable, in that I give myself totally to my mate. I am unclothed physically, emotionally, and practically with one who is not only my partner, but is actually the extension of my own life. As a godly marriage partner, I live graciously, honestly, and openly with my mate. Additionally, I seek to

---

Sidebar:

In this session, be prepared for the couple to potentially be embarrassed and somewhat withdrawn. Ask the Lord to help you be professional and gracious in dealing with the subject of intimacy.

The counselor will bring additional principles and aspects of intimacy to the counseling session. Though it is a difficult subject to approach, it will be necessary to determine the level of sexual intimacy they have already experienced. You must not be tempted to assume they are sexually and morally pure.

If they have been sexually intimate, it will be imperative for them to commit to total abstinence from this moment until their honeymoon.

be creative to discover new and practical ways to communicate to my mate, "Next to the Lord, you are the most important person in the world to me. Therefore, I want to share with you in totality my life, my body, my dreams, my desires, and my love."

Intimacy is always the goal for marriage. Some mistakenly associate the sexual act of marriage as being the only requirement for intimacy. This wonderful gift from God is actually just a part of the closeness of intimacy. There are times when a medical condition may make sexual activity impossible; but intimacy is still achievable for that couple. Intimacy is the closeness and connection that couples can experience even when sexual activity cannot take place. It is built upon trust, security, communication and affection. This intimacy is fresh, growing and of great value. Often, it is manifested with the statement, "My mate is not only my lover, he or she is also my very best friend."

The biblical picture of intimacy takes us back to the Garden of Eden and the experience of Adam with his wife. It will be time well worth the investment to counsel through this very familiar passage.

Adam's placement (Genesis 2:8)

We can only imagine how wonderful the conditions were for Adam. The Lord planted a garden and there He put the man. A "planted garden" and a "put man" describe the amazing situation created by the LORD God. It will be important for the couple to be assured that only Adam's home was planted in such amazingly ideal surroundings. Their home will be planted in the midst of surroundings that are far less than ideal. Therefore the wise couple will determine to seek the Lord's direction and blessing in all of their plans.

Adam's assignment (Genesis 2:15)

Adam had two very important things to do in the Garden. First, he was to dress it. This gives the ideas of laboring or serving. He was to be busy serving in the role of God's worker in an ideal garden. Second, he was to keep it. This gives the idea of watching and waiting as well as being in charge. Adam was to serve and supervise in a beautiful and blessed place.

Adam's aloneness and apartness (Genesis 2:18-20)

An amazing situation was taking place in the ideal garden. Surrounded by beautiful flowers, plants and rivers as well as being in the midst of amazing animals, Adam was not fulfilled or complete. "…But for Adam there was not found an help meet for him" (Genesis 2:20). Something was missing for Adam. God said, "It is not good" (Genesis 2:18a).

Though being placed in a beautiful garden with enjoyable and exciting work, alongside the scores of animals who were without ferociousness, Adam was alone. Within the heart of Adam, the loving Lord God created the desire for closeness and connection. Thus, in an incredible surgical procedure, God took living tissue from the spot that was very near Adam's heart. From this, the Scriptures reveal, "…Made he a woman and brought her unto the man" (Genesis 2:22).

This is an excellent moment to rehearse again how the Lord has brought the couple together. It is so important for the couple to be absolutely certain they can not imagine life without the other. In what ways are they already seeing their role as a "help meet" to their fiancé?

The First Bridal Couple

What must have gone through the mind and heart of Adam when the Lord brought Eve to him? There must have been a sense of supreme joy and amazement in the precious and beautiful provision of the Lord. Moses notes in the context of the marriage in Eden four essential elements of a successful marriage. This is a review from counseling session one. Ask the couple how their understanding of the following four essential elements of a successful marriage has grown throughout the counseling process?

Severance

"Therefore shall a man leave his father and his mother…" (Genesis 2:24a). The idea of leaving is a picture of one untying a shoe string. That which formerly bound us in the child-parent relationship, now is loosened or unbound. It is not that a man deserts his father or mother; rather, he is no longer bound to his parents as when he was a child.

Permanence

"…And shall cleave unto his wife…" (Genesis 2:24b). The word "cleave" is a strong word. It denotes the act of becoming glued, so permanently bonded to another that it cannot be removed without great and lasting damage.

Emphasize once again that marriage is not a contract. Contracts are written in such a way as to provide for loopholes, conditional clauses, and ultimately how to get out of an obligation. Marriage is actually a covenant. The Old Testament Prophet Malachi testified in the strongest of terms to husbands who were sinning. He declared, "…The LORD hath been witness between thee and the wife of thy youth, against whom thou hast dealt treacherously: yet is she thy companion, and the wife of thy covenant" (Malachi 2:14).

As a covenant, couples pledge to each other their lives. There are no provisions for loopholes or clauses to get out of the agreement. Some of the old marriage services actually use the phrase, "I plight thee my troth." Most today would have no idea what a troth plighted would be! Nevertheless, it is imperative to understand the concept of covenant. Adam became glued to his wife. That is intimacy. Married couples today grow in intimacy by understanding the permanence of pledging their life to another and becoming glued to that person.

Closeness

"…And they shall be one flesh" (Genesis 2:24c). One flesh speaks of a unity, closeness and a bond that embraces the emotional, physical and sexual realms. Rather than living under the terms of "me and I," the one-flesh couple develops the "we and us" mentality and lifestyle. This comes from good communication, honesty, and integrity, time shared, common values, and convictions determined, as well as building the marriage upon the Lord Himself.

Intimacy

"And they were both naked, the man and his wife, and were not ashamed" (Genesis 2:25). The concept of not being ashamed contains two elements. First, they were not embarrassed. Second, they were not disappointed. The love Adam and Eve shared with each other was beautifully expressed in Genesis 4:1 with the expression, *"Adam knew Eve his wife…"* The sexual intercourse of Adam and Eve demonstrated their emotional and spiritual closeness as well as the joy shared physically with each other.

The Creator God gave Adam and Eve, as well as married couples throughout the following generations, the same beautiful expression of intimacy. Sexual pleasure and expression within the boundaries of the marriage of the man and woman is part of God's design.

"Marriage is honorable in all and the bed undefiled" (Hebrews 13:4). Such depths of sexual expression and intimacy must never be shared with another as long as life lasts. The Wisdom writer asks a pointed question in Proverbs 5:20: *"Why wilt thou, my son, be ravished with a strange woman, and embrace the bosom of a stranger?"* Sexual intimacy shared only with the marriage partner is that by which great excitement and satisfaction grows.

In the same context as the Wisdom writer's question, comes the writer's observation. *"Drink waters out of thine own cistern, and running waters out of thine own well… Let thy fountain be blessed: and rejoice with the wife of thy youth…Let her breasts satisfy thee at all times; and be thou ravished always with her love"* (Proverbs 5:15-19). Adultery and unfaithfulness will bring great hurt and damage to the marriage. Twenty minutes of passion is never worth the twenty years of pain!

Healthy sexual expression

God has clearly designed men and women to find great fulfillment and satisfaction through the intensely intimate connection of sexuality.

1. Within the boundaries of marriage, sexual love is a gift from God and is therefore honorable (Hebrews 13:4).
2. Sex is not to be selfishly sought for one's own pleasure; but rather it is given as a token and demonstration of love for one's partner.
3. Sexual activity is intended to bring fulfillment and satisfaction to both partners. Therefore it is not to be given as a reward, nor is it to be withheld as punishment.
4. As the fulfillment of a closeness being built into the marriage, wise couples talk about their sexual experience. The husband and wife who share a healthy concept of their sexuality understand that the act of marriage requires practice and patience with each other.

The wife has the need to be loved and cherished. She is aroused much more slowly (some would suggest it begins in the kitchen as the husband helps with dishes!) and needs time to prepare for the bedroom. Physical touch, tender words and the assurance she is cherished will prepare her for intimacy.

Quite the opposite, the man is aroused by thought and sight. He is ready for intimacy much more quickly than his wife. Both partners must understand their mate and desire to be thoughtful, caring, loving, and sexually giving in their marriage. Godly husbands learn to be gentle, loving, affectionate and demonstrative in cherishing their wives.

On the other hand, a godly wife knows her husband has very strong sexual drives. She loves her husband and is thankful she can express her love for him and finds joy in freely giving herself to him. Healthy sexual attitudes are built upon the fact that the partners no longer have claim to their own bodies. Rather, in love and tenderness, both give their bodies to each other (1 Corinthians 7:4). In the mutual giving, there is mutual satisfaction.

Several books could be suggested at this point in the counseling process. Among the many possibilities (without the author's recommendation or endorsement), the pastor-counselor could recommend the following:

> *The Honeymoon of Your Dreams* by Walt Larimore and Susan Crockett, Regal Books, 2005.
> *The Act of Marriage* by Tim and Beverly LaHaye, Zondervan Publishing House, 1998.
> *Intended for Pleasure* by Ed and Gayle Wheat, Fleming H. Revell Publishers, 1997.

Danger! Intimacy Can Be Damaged and Destroyed!

Intimacy is much more than just sexual intercourse. While sex is great, the whole concept of intimacy is far greater. Intimacy is the closeness that results from a couple being glued together sexually as well as emotionally.

Within every marriage, dangers lurk nearby which consistently damage the closeness and intimacy of marriage. While the following is not an exhaustive list, these are the typical dangers that damage and destroy marriages.

Expectations not fulfilled

An expectation is that which is established in the mind of a person as to certainties or demands. It is something anticipated or looked forward to. While some expectations are reasonable, many are not. Several common unrealistic expectations in marriage would include the following:

- My husband is not only going to love me; he will be romantic every day in the way he treats me.
- My wife is going to cook for me just exactly like my mother cooks.
- My husband is going to appreciate all my efforts and will tell me often how special I am.
- My wife will always be ready for sex when I suggest it.

- My husband will be thoughtful of my feelings and will speak tenderly to me even when he is frustrated.
- My wife will always respect my leadership and will encourage me even when I am or she is having a hard day.
- My husband will tell me about all the details of his day. He will love to share with me at length about everything.
- My wife will understand that I want a little quietness and relaxation without talking all evening long.

It will be very wise to probe into the couple's expectations. While not limited to this list, these things will provide a good beginning to understanding expectations. When expectations are not fulfilled, a wedge is created and closeness is damaged.

Promises not fulfilled

Emergencies can unexpectedly change the best-laid plans, in a great hurry! Explain the difference between the infrequent emergency and the consistently broken promise that shatters intimacy.

Ultimately, the Lord Himself is the only one who has never broken a promise (1Kings 8:56). Promises fulfilled are not only the rule of a healthy marriage; they are the characteristic of genuine Christianity (Romans 12:17). Broken promises relating to dates, activities, shared experiences, and family living are huge wedges that destroy closeness.

Conflicts not resolved

Think of it. Here are two people, living independently of each other for several decades, coming from different backgrounds, with different personalities and different preferences uniting to form a relationship that is characterized by "one flesh" in nature. Conflicts are inevitable. Unresolved conflicts grow and fester, resulting in serious damage to the closeness of the marriage. These are among the typically unresolved conflicts that damage intimacy.

- How frequently do we hope to have sexual activity in the week?
- Who will handle the checkbook, and how we will spend our money? (If the financial planner has not been completed before, this is a good time to review it.)
- How soon will we start our family?
- How often will we visit each other's family?
- What are the things we really need in our home?
- How many children do we wish to raise?
- What are the duties we want our mate to fulfill?
- How do we want our home to be kept, and how do we want it to look?
- How much should we save and put away for emergencies and retirement?
- What will we do in our leisure time?
- How will she know she is cherished?
- How will he know he is respected?
- Will both partners work after the baby comes?

Schedules and time not wisely managed

Most couples are busy. Many are too busy. If there is not sufficient time for worship, work, service, recreation and family, the schedule is overloaded.

Time management is better understood as the wise handling of God's time. The Lord owns or possesses everything, including time. As stewards, we must be faithful in the way we manage time and handle the many potential activities that come (1 Corinthians 4:2).

Couples who enjoy a growing intimacy give first priority to the Lord Jesus. He is the object of their worship, praise and obedience. Worship comes first in the daily priority of wise stewards.

Even though work is a major activity in the stewardship of time, it must never become the idol demanding more and more allegiance and investment. A huge and dangerous trap to be avoided by those couples who grow in intimacy is the overly demanding pressure and temptation to expend undue time to accumulate more riches. Those who set riches as the ultimate priority open themselves to great harm and hurt (1Timothy 6:6-10).

Family time provides the opportunity to reconnect after a busy day in the work world. Although most couples need a few minutes of quietness and personal time, wise couples enjoy being together, talking with each other, playing together and sharing experiences, even in the very common and routine matters such as running errands. This is called connection and is a necessary component of emotional intimacy.

Actions and attitudes that are not thoughtful

Remind the couple that in many ways marriage is very much like a bank. Every action that is helpful, blessed, encouraging and uplifting is similar to making a deposit in the bank. Likewise the thoughtless or hurtful action, which should be very infrequent, is comparable to making withdrawals. Obviously, healthy bank accounts have larger deposits than withdrawals. The same is true in marriages.

A careful reading of 1 Corinthians 13 clearly defines actions that are loving, thoughtful and kind. The couple who would enjoy intimacy in their marriage are those who live out the description of the Apostle as he wrote to the Corinthian believers. Imagine the closeness in marriage that comes when husbands and wives are committed to the following principles:

- Love is patient
- Love is kind
- Love does not envy
- Love does not boast
- Love is not proud
- Love is not rude
- Love is not self-seeking
- Love is not easily angered
- Love keeps no record or list of wrong-doing

> You have been counseling in very intimate areas with the couple. This session provides a good opportunity for the pastor-counselor to stop and reflect upon his own marriage. In the extreme busyness of schedule and demands of ministry, how is your marriage doing in the intimacy area?

- Love does not delight in evil, but rejoices with the truth
- Love always protects and trusts
- Love hopes and perseveres
- Love never fails

There will be many additional thoughts and principles you as the counselor may wish to add to this session. As you conclude, it will be interesting to note the questions the couple may have as relating to sexuality. Keep in mind several things.

1. It is wise to suggest to the bride that she should schedule a gynecological visit. While it is rare, occasionally she may require a minor surgical procedure. Certainly if she is going to use birth control methods requiring a prescription, she will need such an appointment. Be sure in her appointment, she makes it clear to the physician that she desires to prevent pregnancy, not terminate it.
2. Do not assume the couple already are familiar with the mechanics and facts of sexual expression. Many couples who have remained virgins are very unfamiliar with what to expect, how to prepare, and what to do in sexual activity. As the pastor-counselor, you have a great opportunity to dispel fears, correct false assumptions and provide personal and practical direction for the couple.

Take as much time as necessary for this session. In fact, if needed, you may wish to schedule an additional time with this couple. There is nothing as precious as the couple who experiences the intimate blessing of the Song of Solomon 2:16, "My beloved is mine and I am his."

The Final Session

Finally you have walked the bridal couple through the gamut of premarital counseling. At this point, the next wonderful task will be to plan the actual wedding ceremony. The couple's edition of *From This Day Forward* contains the three sample wedding ceremonies found in the next chapter. While a few may wish to write their own ceremony, or at least their own vows, many will choose to use one of the ceremonies you offer. The next chapter will provide you with several selections as well as wedding features.

Send the couple home with the copies of the wedding services you offer. Ask them to fill in the blanks of "Our Wedding Ceremony" or you may do this yourself in person during the next counseling session.

Chapter Seven—Counseling Session 7

The Ceremony— Helping the Couple Plan Their Special Day

There is a sense of joy and accomplishment as a task comes to a completion. What a huge task indeed as the pastor-counselor prepares the couple for the journey of a lifetime! Now comes the final counseling session before the wedding, when the couple will have one more opportunity to counsel with you through any additional situations. Also, they will plan the wedding ceremony with you as the officiating pastor. What a great privilege is afforded the counseling pastor as you guide the couple in producing a ceremony that is truly meaningful to them and glorifying to the Lord.

Goals for this Session

1. Communicate to the couple your desire to address any fears, questions, concerns or situations that are yet unresolved. It will be wise to review several of the areas in which you know the couple is working. How are they progressing in these areas?
2. Check for indications of readiness for marriage such as specific areas in which they have prayed, talked and arrived at a decision or conclusion.
3. Secure the details for their wedding ceremony and reception. Ask the Lord for wisdom as to how to address questionable ideas the couple may wish to incorporate into their wedding festivities. Occasionally because of biblical convictions, pastors may have to redirect some of the wishes of the couple.

Begin the Session

Hopefully by now, you as the pastor-counselor have become very familiar with this couple. There are several questions you must ask yourself and the couple. You may have additional questions you may wish to jot down in the margin. Additionally be sure to include these questions now in your final scheduled counseling session before the wedding.

1. Do both possess a strong testimony of personal faith in the Lord Jesus Christ? If so, are they growing spiritually?
2. Does the groom demonstrate the characteristics of being a godly, loving spiritual leader? Does the bride demonstrate the biblical characteristics of a godly wife who respects and loves her husband?

3. Are the areas of conflict that surfaced in earlier counseling sessions being addressed and resolution taking place?
4. Are both families happy with the upcoming marriage? Has any situation developed in which you as the pastor should be made aware?
5. Are there any other questions or concerns that must be addressed?

Biblical counseling is comparable to a shepherd who spends time with his individual sheep. The purpose of the shepherd is very direct, targeting the individual needs of the sheep and addressing them. Carefully checking for sickness or injuries, the wise shepherd out of love and concern for the sheep, takes to heart what will be best for his flock. Likewise, the biblical counselor always has the glory of the Lord and the good of the couple at heart.

Following the final items of specific counseling, it is time now to review the plan the couple has for the wedding ceremony. Every ceremony should be unique to the couple. It will be a blessing to counsel through with the couple several principles to remember.

> On some occasions one or both families may be somewhat unhappy about the wedding. Wise pastors at least listen to their objections or concerns before proceeding with the wedding plans.

A Godly Wedding Ceremony

In a wonderful way, Christ adorned the wedding at Cana (John 2) with his personal presence. A valid reminder to the couple as they begin their new life together and establish their godly home is the commitment to make their wedding and reception (which will be discussed in the next chapter) a God-honoring and glorifying celebration. Several things to keep in mind in establishing a godly wedding and reception would include the following:

1. Often unsaved family and friends attend the believer's wedding when otherwise they would not attend a preaching service. A great opportunity for planting an evangelistic seed is possible in the godly wedding. With the couple's permission, present the gospel clearly.
2. Tactfully and tenderly filter out items that are not biblical or godly. Ask to see and hear the special music that is being selected. Beware of special readings that may be requested by the couple in the wedding service. More than a few pastors have been surprised when suddenly an uncle wishes to read something, or someone suggests something to be read. Be prepared to review every aspect of the ceremony. As the pastor, you are in charge (even if a wedding coordinator is enlisted) of all the activities of the day.
3. If the couple wishes to use a ceremony different from what you will offer, graciously insist you must read it as soon as possible. Very few couples are writers. Most will not desire to write their own ceremony. However, for those who do wish to write the vows, occasionally a pastor will find it necessary to help them rethink and reword some of their statements.
4. This is a celebration of two families who love their children and are coming together before the Lord and the presence of friends to witness the establishment of a godly home and family. The couple is not entering a contract; but rather a covenant and companionship (Malachi 2:14). The vows are significant and must be highlighted and emphasized. For these to be established, the couple must genuinely seek the Lord and invite Him to be part of the entire day.

> Many pastors have taken the stand that they will not perform the ceremony of any couple who will have alcoholic beverages served at the reception. This is based on the conviction that alcohol is a leading enemy of the home. Each pastor using this handbook will have to develop his own convictions and establish policies within his own local church.

With this in view, this chapter will present the counseling pastor with a suggested form to be completed to list all the wedding details. Also, several wedding ceremonies written by the author are presented and are available to be used in the wedding ceremony. (Permission is granted to run copies of the Wedding Details.)

Wedding Details for the Couple and Pastor

Groom's full name _____

Bride's full name _____

Date of wedding _____ Time _____

Maid/Matron of Honor _____

Maids attending: _____

_____

_____

Best Man _____

Ushers: _____

_____

_____

Flower Girl _____

Ring Bearer _____

Organist _____

Special music: _____

_____

Wedding service selected _____

Wedding Coordinator _____

Florist _____

Photographer _____

Date of wedding rehearsal _____ Time _____

Approximate number attending wedding _____

Special features to be included in the ceremony_____

_____

_____

Master of Ceremonies at reception _____

From This Day Forward

Do we use a wedding coordinator?

Based on Ephesians 4:12, pastors are to labor tirelessly in equipping the saints for ministry. Godly pastors do not function alone in performing ministry; rather they train believers to do the work of the ministry.

One such ministry is that of the wedding coordinator. More than a few pastors have experienced the feelings of being frazzled as he, the groom and the ushers nervously stand in an adjacent room in the front of the auditorium wondering what was happening awaiting the delayed beginning of the wedding. At precisely 1:00 the organist was to play "O Perfect Love" signifying the candles were lit and the bride was ready. It is now 1:07 and no "O Perfect Love!" What does the pastor do now? His options are to peek out the door, walk down a side aisle trying to act like this is part of the plan, or just wait it out with the anxious groom and his attendants. None of those options are pleasant.

A wedding coordinator can be of great benefit not only in getting everyone in the right place at the right time, but also in assisting the pastor with many details of the wedding and ceremony. Professional wedding coordinators are hired to be in charge and carry out the wishes and contractual agreement with the bride (and her parents who are paying for the wedding). The professionally hired coordinator operates within the budget and secures all the venues of the wedding, including the church and minister. In this sense, most couples will not find it necessary to expend such a sum of money on a professional coordinator.

The pastor must be in charge of the ceremony, facilities and activities. However, wise pastors have found great benefits and rewards in training at least one willing lady to serve as wedding coordinator. She must be a godly believer, of strong conviction and values, possessing a good reputation within the church congregation and one who works well with the pastor. Friendliness, tactfulness, organizational skills, administration and being given to details are among the qualities of a good wedding coordinator.

The responsibilities of the biblical wedding coordinator include but are not limited to the following:

1. The Wedding Coordinator (WC) will be contacted by either the bride or pastor at least four months before the wedding date to ensure she is available on the date selected for the wedding.
2. The WC will meet with the bride (and possibly the mother of the bride) to review the details of the wedding and reception. The WC will advise the bride and give suggestions that will help the wedding ceremony and reception to function smoothly.
3. The WC will work closely with the bride and her family, being available to supervise the setting up of the reception as well as being the point person for the florist, photographer, wedding cake baker, caterer, video technician, sound room technician, and attendants. She oversees the arrival of the wedding attendants, the changing rooms, floral arrangements, guest book placement, and double-checks on the special arrangements of the wedding ceremony.

4. In most local church weddings, the bride's family will enlist help to set up for the reception as well as the cleanup that follows. The WC will be available to make suggestions or offer help with these details.
5. The WC will assist the pastor in the rehearsal of the ceremony. Each pastor will decide how much of the responsibility of the wedding rehearsal will fall to the WC. Some pastors prefer being in charge of the rehearsal with the WC being primarily responsible for ensuring the bridal party is lined up and ready for the ceremony at the appointed time.

    Other pastors prefer to have the WC oversee more of the rehearsal. While the pastor is in attendance and will rehearse the wedding ceremony with the couple, in this case the WC will rehearse with the attendants the role of the ushers, their placement in the processional as well as in the ceremony, the coordinating of the preliminary music, and the details such as lighting of the candles, extending the runner, and special music before the wedding ceremony begins.
6. Even if the pastor prefers not to enlist and train a WC, it is advisable to have a trusted and administrative lady to be in the back of the auditorium with the bridal party to ensure that all members are ready for the ceremony to begin. This relieves much pressure on the pastor who is far in location from the bride and her attendants without the possibility of communication.

> The author gives permission to the pastors to use any of these samples as written. If an officiating pastor wishes to rewrite any portion of these samples, please contact Dr. Michael Peck at Baptist Church Planters for permission.
>
> Special features may be added without seeking the author's permission.

Wedding ceremonies available to be used

Three wedding samples are offered which are very basic in design. In the next chapter, many special features are included which will help to create a ceremony that will be a blessing as well as a testimony to those who attend. Additionally, the couple may have special features unique to themselves they wish to include in the ceremony.

Wedding Ceremony Sample 1

The Processional

What a wonderful God to whom we believers belong! He is referred to by many names and characteristics in the Bible. Perhaps the most beautiful of all His names is the personal name, Yahweh, Jehovah. This is the amazing personal name that means He is the self-existent One, the eternal God Himself. Unlike His creation, our God is self-sufficient. He needs no one else to survive and to exist. Yet, incredibly, in eternity past, the Father, Son, and Holy Spirit made a beautiful and incredibly amazing decision. They would reveal themselves and create man.

Thus into the beautiful flowers of the Garden of Eden, God created and placed Adam, the first man. Adam the man was the crown of all God's creation. He was given the garden to explore, dress and keep for the Lord. Work was to be totally enjoyable there in the beautiful, weedless, sinless garden. Adam also enjoyed the friendship of the animals. With no ferociousness, Adam sensed no fear as he mingled with the incredible animal kingdom. Most amazing of all, Adam must have sensed great joy as he experienced the fellowship of Jehovah God.

Yet dear friends, something was missing. The Bible records the Lord's statement in Genesis 2:18, "It is not good that the man should be alone; I will make him an help meet for him." God already knew that something was missing in Adam's life. He gave Adam the opportunity and time to make such a discovery for himself. Hence, God performed the first surgery and removed living tissue from the side of Adam. This tissue was not from his head to rule over her, nor from his feet to trample her under; but from his side. This tissue was taken from the spot closest to heart of Adam, his very rib. This demonstrates that Eve was to be close to him. At his side, beautifully equal in value, she was to be cherished and loved. She was his companion, his help meet.

As Adam awoke from the surgery, a beautiful sight awaited him, as recorded in Genesis 2:22. The Bible declares that God brought her unto the man. Adam's first moments of consciousness must have been joyous. Now he had a sweet addition to his formerly lonely life; Eve was the cherished partner of God's choosing.

Today before this assembled congregation, another re-enactment of the Lord's working is taking place as He brings (Bride's name) and (Groom's name) together in marriage. It is special to remember that God Himself officiated at the first of all the wedding ceremonies. He blessed the marriage of Adam and Eve with His own presence. Likewise today, the Lord is here with us and earnestly desires to bless this marriage and home.

Prayer

Counsel

To the Groom: (Groom's name), as Adam was not fulfilled apart from Eve, so you will never find true fulfillment apart from (Bride's name). Not only is your wedding a picture of what the Lord did in the garden of Eden, even greater it is a vivid picture of the relationship between Christ and His church. When you love your wife as the Bible commands, you will love her even as Christ loved the church and gave Himself for it. While you may never have the opportunity of laying down your life for your wife, you certainly can live for her each day. May Christ Himself aide and assist you in becoming the kind of husband He wants you to be. (Groom's name), may you be strong of character, deep in courage, consistent in conviction, great in tenderness and excellent in your devoted love and considerate treatment of your wife. She is God's precious gift to you.

To the Bride: (Bride's name), As Eve was brought to Adam long ago to be his help meet, may you find a great sense of joy in your role as partner, friend, counselor, lover and encourager. A help meet is one that is just right, perfectly suitable for her partner. Thus, may the Lord give you a special love and respect for your husband.

The submission of the wife as commanded in the Scriptures is not the submission of dread and fear; but of love, joy and respect. Make your husband your best friend and serve the Lord together as partners. May you be godly in character, faithful in living, and gracious in your love for Christ and your husband.

Presentation of the Bride

To the Father: Dad, what a special time for you and your wife. The years of training, nurturing and teaching bring you to this joyous moment. Do you and your wife this day present your daughter to be married to this man? Father replies, "Yes, her mother and I do." (Father kisses daughter and shakes the hand of the groom as he welcomes him into his family. Father is seated.)

Vows

To the Groom: (Groom's name), before the Lord I am now asking you in the presence of these witnesses, do you willingly and joyfully take (Bride's name) to be your own precious wife? Do you promise this day that you will love her, honor her, protect her, cherish her, and give yourself always to your wife, as a godly husband should? Groom replies: "I do."

To the Bride: (Bride's name), before the Lord I am now asking you in the presence of these witnesses, do you willingly and joyfully take (Groom's name) to be your own precious husband? Do you promise this day that you will love him, honor him, and cherish him, even as a godly wife should? Bride replies: "I do."

At this point if the Bride is carrying a floral arrangement, she will pass it to her maid/matron of honor.

To the Couple: You have promised that you are joyfully taking each other as husband and wife. Would you now join your right hands? The beautiful symbolism of the right hand in the Old Testament demonstrated strength and might. Today as you join your right hands, you are joining together in a new and beautiful strength.

These vows are for a lifetime. The promises you are making are unconditional. Together you are pledging your lives in a loving covenant of strength and beauty. Malachi 2:14 states "…she is your companion and the wife of your covenant."

To the Groom: (The groom turns and faces his bride to repeat his vows.) Please repeat your vows after me. "I (Groom's name) take you (Bride's name)… to be my own… wedded wife. I love you… with all of my heart…and I pledge to you…that I will seek…to become the husband…God wants me to be. I cherish you…and commit myself to you. This commitment is for better or worse… richer or poorer…in sickness and in health…as long as life shall last. I pledge to you… my life and love."

To the Bride: (The bride still facing her groom to repeat her vows.) Please repeat your vows after me. "I (Bride's name) take you (Groom's name)…to be my own…wedded husband. I love you with all of my heart. I pledge to you…I will seek to become…the wife God wants me to be. I cherish you… and commit myself to you. This commitment is for better or worse… richer or poorer…in sickness and in health…as long as life shall last. I pledge to you…my life and love."

The Exchanging of the Rings

The vows just repeated are both beautiful and lasting. (Groom's name) and (Bride's name) have pledged to each other their life and love. Now we come to the moment in the ceremony where the rings are placed on the ring finger of the bride and groom. These rings are the outward and visible symbol of the vows just repeated. Daily the couple will see their wedding rings and will be reminded of this very special moment when they pledged to each other their life and love.

To the Groom: (Groom's name) please place the ring on your bride's ring finger and repeat after me, "I place this ring…on your finger…to constantly remind you…of the love I have for you…and the promise of my life. With this ring…I marry you today."

To the Bride: (Bride's name) please place the ring on your groom's ring finger and repeat after me, "I place this ring…on your finger…to constantly remind you…of the love I have for you…and the promise of my life. With this ring…I marry you today."

The Pronouncement

For as much then, as you (Groom's full name and Bride's full name) have joyfully entered this marriage and have pledged your total commitment to each other, I therefore by the authority vested in me as a minister of the Lord Jesus Christ, pronounce you husband and wife.

The Lord Jesus Himself said "What therefore God hath joined together, let not man put asunder" according to Matthew 19:6. (Groom's name and Bride's name) let no difficulty, no disappointment, no obstacle ever divide you asunder. Do not allow any person to come between you. May the love you have for each other this day continue to grow and blossom. As the Lord allows, may you have many years together and may you have the joy of growing old together. May the peace of Christ and the joy of the Lord mark your home. The Psalmist of old declared in Psalm 128:1, "Blessed is every one that feareth the LORD; that walketh in his ways."

May the Lord bless you and keep you. May the Lord make His face to shine upon you and be gracious unto you. May the Lord give you joy and peace as you walk with Him each day.

Prayer

The husband may now kiss his wife.

The Presentation

(The couple turns and faces the congregation as the bride takes her floral arrangement once again.) Now, it is my very happy privilege to introduce and present to you, Mr. and Mrs. (Name).

The Recessional

Wedding Ceremony Sample 2

The Processional

The Welcome: Dear family and friends of (Groom's name) and dear family and friends of (Bride's name), we come together today to celebrate this very special moment. It is our privilege to hear the vows they will make to each other as well as witness the giving and receiving of the wedding rings. We will share in the joy of the pronouncement of their marriage. On behalf of the bride and groom, welcome and thank you for sharing in this most joyous occasion.

Marriage, home and family are God's idea and plan. In the beautiful Garden of Eden, God brought Eve to Adam to be his help meet, his companion, and his completion. Christ Himself performed His first miracle at the wedding of Cana. The Apostle Paul declared marriage to be honorable. The home was God's very first institution. We come today with joy and excitement as we share this very special occasion with two people we love. Let us begin the service with prayer and ask the Lord's blessing.

Prayer

Charge to Couple

(Groom's name and Bride's name), it is a blessing to gather today to celebrate your marriage. This day marks a new beginning in your lives. A brand-new home will be established in the next few moments. The Lord has wonderfully worked in your lives and brought you together for a lifetime. You are about to exchange vows that are best understood as the pledging of your life. These vows are not contracts which can be broken or renegotiated. Rather, you are entering a covenant, a lifelong pledge of giving yourselves to each other. This marriage covenant is for a lifetime. The Lord wants to bless your marriage and home with His grace and help.

The Presentation

To the Father: Dad, you and your wife rejoiced when your daughter was born. As parents, you taught her to walk. Then you taught her to ride a bicycle. Next you taught her to drive a car. Probably the years have flown by very quickly for you. Now your life enters the next dimension as you bring your daughter to this man to be his wife. Is it your intention this day to give your daughter in marriage to this man? Father replies: Yes, Her mother and I do. (Father kisses daughter and shakes hand of groom welcoming him to his family. Father is seated.)

No other ties compare to the bonding as husband and wife. No other vows are more significant than what you are about to make. The Lord Jesus Christ and your family and friends rejoice in what you are about to promise.

To the Groom: (Groom's name), do you this day take this woman to become your own wedded wife? Do you promise to establish a home that is godly, and do you promise to live with your wife as a loving spiritual leader who is pleasing to the Lord? Do you promise to love her, cherish her, provide for her, and protect her? Do you pledge to her your love and life? Groom replies: "I do."

To the Bride: (Bride's name), do you this day take this man to become your own wedded husband? Do you promise to establish a home that is godly, and do you promise to live with your husband as a loving spiritual wife? Do you promise to love him, cherish him, serve with him as his partner and be a wife that is pleasing to the Lord? Do you pledge to him your love and life? Bride replies: "I do."

The Reading of Ephesians 5:21-33

(A greeting from the bridal couple, either from the groom himself, or by the pastor on their behalf is given at this point. Following this, a brief presentation of the gospel is appropriate at this point in the service.)

I will now ask the bride and groom to face each other and hold their hands. (If the bride is carrying a floral arrangement, she will pass it to the maid/matron of honor.) You have indicated your desire to become husband and wife. The Song of Solomon 2:16 declares, "My beloved is mine, and I am his…" This speaks of oneness, closeness and a joy in knowing you belong to each other. These vows you are about to make are the pledges of your lifetime.

To the Groom: (Groom's name), you will repeat your vows after me, "I (Groom's name) take you (Bride's name)… to be my wedded wife. I pledge my life to you… to have and to hold…from this day forward. I freely give my love to you…in days that are better or worse…times when we are richer or poorer…in cases of sickness or health…for the rest of my life. I pledge this to you…as your own husband."

To the Bride: (Bride's name), you will repeat your vows after me, "I (Bride's name) take you (Groom's name)to be my wedded husband. I pledge my life to you…to have and to hold…from this day forward. I freely give my love to you…in days that are better or worse…times when we are richer or poorer…in cases of sickness or health…for the rest of my life. I pledge this to you…as your own wife."

The Exchanging of the Rings

The wedding ring is a beautiful symbol of the vows that were just exchanged. Every day the couple will see their rings and remember once again what they have promised. The wedding ring displayed announces that I belong to another. My life is no longer my own. I am married and have pledged my life, love and loyalty to my beloved.

To the Groom: You will repeat after me as you place the ring upon the bride's ring finger. "With this ring… I now marry you… and pledge to you… my constant trust…and abiding love."

To the Bride: You will repeat after me as you place the ring upon the groom's ring finger. "With this ring… I now marry you… and pledge to you… my constant trust…and abiding love."

May these rings given and received be the constant reminder of your love and devotion to each other and may the Lord abundantly bless your marriage.

The Pronouncement

For as much as (Groom's full name) and (Bride's full name) have consented to marriage and have confirmed this by declaring it in vows and exchanging of wedding rings, by the authority committed unto me as a minister of the Lord Jesus Christ and the state of (name of state), I now therefore pronounce you husband and wife.

Closing Charge

Dearly beloved, this day marks a brand-new beginning in your lives now united. You are no longer single. No longer is it me, myself and I. Now today marks the start of the journey of a lifetime as husband and wife. The words "us" and "we" will become the new normal. Keep Christ first in your lives, marriage, and home. Seek His blessing in every thing you do. Ask His direction in every decision ahead. Make Him the Lord of your household. May the desire of your heart be the same as Joshua as he declared, "But as for me and my house, we will serve the Lord" (Joshua 24:15).

Prayer

(Groom's name), you may now kiss your new wife.

Presentation and Introduction

(Minister suggests that the couple turn and face the congregation. Bride takes her floral arrangement from the maid/matron of honor). Families and friends, it is now my joyous privilege to introduce and present to you, Mr. and Mrs. (full name).

Recessional

Wedding Ceremony Sample 3

The Processional

The Welcome

Dear family and friends, on behalf of (Names of Groom and Bride) I would like to welcome you and thank you for coming today. What an incredible day this is to this dear couple as well as to the Lord Jesus Christ, to the parents of the bride and groom, and to each of you as family and friends.

As the seasons of the year come and go, likewise there are seasons in our lives. To the parents, it probably seems like such a short time ago you held your babies in your arms as you dreamed of what their lives would be like. You saw them take their first really wobbly steps. When they skinned their knee, you were there to kiss it and make it all better.

You taught them how to ride a bike, skip a stone across the water, and make a kite. Before you knew it, Kindergarten came, and you couldn't believe it when they graduated from high school. Now today, you are part of a very great day in their lives. Two individual people, uniquely designed by an all wise and loving Lord, each with their own distinct personalities, backgrounds, and talents, come to be united in marriage.

The Bible says in Genesis 2:24 and 25, "Therefore shall a man leave his father and his mother and shall cleave unto his wife: and they shall be one flesh. And they were both naked, the man his wife, and were not ashamed." Modern day philosophy says, "I am the most important person in the whole world. I deserve to be happy and therefore my great purpose is to please myself." But for the believing couple, the greatest joy in all of life is together seeking to please the Lord and love one another for a life time.

This love is a very special love. It is called *agape* love. The Lord Jesus said, "Greater love hath no man than this, that a man lay down his life for his friends" (John 15:13). This love is a decision of your will, that you will consistently and devotedly seek the well-being of the other. Such love will bring joy to your home and blessing to your lives. This kind of love will face the greatest adversities, resolve the deepest conflicts and survive the greatest storms. When you as a couple love one another and become one flesh, home will be a blessing and your marriage will be precious. This love will deepen as you grow older together.

To the Father: Dad, the little girl you held in your arms is now a beautiful lady. Is it the intention of you and your wife to bring your daughter to this man for marriage today? Father replies: "Her mother and I give our blessing." (Father kisses his daughter, shakes the hand of the groom, and joins their hands in the aisle before being seated.)

Today is a blending of that which is a celebration and that which is sacred and serious. We celebrate the goodness of God and His precious

Chapter 7 67

provision of each for the other. As family and friends, we share together many wonderful and often humorous experiences. The reception will be a time marked with remembering and rejoicing.

On the other hand, this couple is about to pledge to each other their lives. This moment marks the solemn and lifelong commitment to one another. (Names of Groom and Bride), you are entering into the making of a lifelong covenant. You are pledging to each other a mutual trust and devotion, never to be shared with another as long as life shall last. We are witnesses together of this precious and powerful moment.

To the Groom: (Name of Groom), do you realize what a treasure you have been given by the Lord? The writer of Proverbs states, "Who can find a virtuous woman? for her price is far above rubies" (Proverbs 31:10). When you view your wife as a treasure far above the value of rubies, you then begin to understand the gift God has given to you. Treasure her. Thank the Lord for her. Be to her a godly husband. When you love your wife in the same manner as Christ loves His church, your life will never be the same. Such love in your heart will help you to determine to be the loving, gentle and godly spiritual leader in your home. Such love will help you through any situation. May God bless your role of husband. May you live in such a way as to never violate the trust your wife has in you.

To the Bride: (Name of Bride), throughout the Scriptures, precious ladies have found great joy and blessing in being united to their husbands and lovingly them tenderly and devotedly. Of Eve, the Scriptures record that God brought her unto the man. Imagine the joy and anticipation Rebekah had when the Scriptures speak of her becoming Isaac's wife and his love for her. Over and over the love story is repeated. Ruth and Boaz, Abigail and David, Mary and Joseph are among the many. Today you join a precious company of godly ladies blessed by the Lord and loved by their husbands. May God bless your role of wife. May you live in such a way as to never violate the trust your husband has in you.

Prayer

Scripture: Matthew 19:5-6

The Vows

This moment marks the pledging of each other for a lifetime. Far beyond a contract which can be broken and renegotiated, this covenant pledges the lives of the husband and wife to each other as long as life lasts.

(The minister suggests the bride give her floral arrangement to the maid/matron of honor, and the couple turns, facing each other and holding hands.)

To the Groom: (Name of Groom), if it is your intention to enter into the marriage vows, then you will repeat the following after me. "I (Name of Groom), rejoice in God's blessing…and His gift to me. I pledge my love and life…to you (Name of Bride)… and will be faithful to you…honor and love you…protect and cherish you…as long as life shall last. I give to you… the pledge of my love…in days of sickness and health… days of being richer or poorer…for better or worse. I am yours."

To the Bride: (Name of Bride), if it is your intention to enter into the marriage vows, then you will repeat the following after me. "I (Name of Bride), rejoice in God's blessing… and His gift to me. I pledge my love and life… to you (Name of Groom)… and will be faithful to you…I will honor and love you… and keep myself only for you… as long as life shall last. I give to you… the pledge of my love…in days of sickness and health… days of being richer or poorer… for better or worse. I am yours."

The Exchanging of the Rings

This couple has entered into a lifelong covenant together. We are witnesses of these joyous vows. Now comes the exchanging of the rings which is the outward, visible symbol of the promise just made.

To the Groom: (Name of Groom), you will place the ring on your bride's ring finger and repeat the following after me. "(Name of Bride), I give you this ring… as the token of my pledge. May it constantly remind us… of our promise and joy. I take you as my precious wife."

To the Bride: (Name of Bride), you will place the ring on your groom's ring finger and repeat the following after me. "(Name of Groom), I give you this ring… as the token of my pledge. May it constantly remind us… of our promise and joy. I take you as my precious husband."

The Pronouncement

Today (Groom's full name) and (Bride's full name) have presented themselves before this company of witnesses and have each pledged their lives to the other. They have exchanged rings as visible tokens of this enduring pledge. Therefore, by the authority vested in me as a minister of the Lord Jesus Christ and by the state of _____, I now pronounce you to be husband and wife. What God has joined together, let no man divide asunder.

Closing Benediction

A brand-new home has just been established. May the joy of the presence of Christ, the authority of the Word of God, and the fellowship that comes when two people are devoted to the Lord characterize your lives. May your home be godly. May your lives grow closer to each other and to the Lord who dearly loves you both. May the Lord bless and keep you in the days and years ahead.

(Name of Groom), you may now kiss your new wife.

Introduction and Presentation

(The minister now suggests the couple turn and face the congregation as the bride takes her floral arrangement from the maid/matron of honor.) Now it is my very happy privilege to introduce and present to you, Mr. and Mrs. (Name).

Recessional

****

May the Lord give you wisdom in superintending the wedding ceremony as well as grace as you work with the bridal couple. At times, various individuals will share their opinions and suggestions at the wedding rehearsal. Always conform to the wishes of the bridal couple worked out ahead of time with you as the officiating pastor.

Chapter Eight—Special Features

Making the Ceremony Unique

It is not uncommon to discover that the bride has dreamed of this day for many years. She may indeed come with more than just a few ideas and suggestions of what she wants for the wedding ceremony. Usually pastors are happy to incorporate these ideas into the wedding ceremony whenever possible. Sometimes the bridal couple, though excited about their marriage, will not have a lot of suggestions or ideas concerning the ceremony.

With this in mind, a wonderful opportunity exists to help the couple create a unique and beautiful ceremony. Several biblical principles must be kept in mind in preparing the ceremony.

1. This is a time to glorify the Lord Jesus (1 Corinthians 10:31). While we are to glorify Him in everything we do, this is a very special opportunity to greatly honor Him.
2. A great opportunity exists to be a witness to unsaved friends and family who will be assembled (Mark 16:15). This may be one of the few times unsaved family and friends will come to church and be exposed to the gospel.
3. Since many marriages struggle today, the wedding ceremony presents the possibility of genuine ministry to hurting couples. Therefore the wedding ceremony must be worthy of the Lord (Colossians 1:10).

> This chapter provides the officiating pastor with creative ideas to be offered to the bridal party for their wedding. Permission is granted to use any of these features. If any changes in the readings are desired, permission from the author must be arranged.

The following special features will focus on three areas of the wedding ceremony. First, what can take place in the moments just before the wedding ceremony begins? Second, think about the processional. How will the bridal party enter the service? Third, what are the typical as well as unique features that can be added to the ceremony to make it truly spiritual?

The Moments Just before the Wedding Ceremony Begins

Traditionally, the wedding ceremony begins with the seating of the bride's mother. This is a special moment in the service signifying the bride is ready and the ceremony begins. Several very special features are possible during these moments.

Music

The bride, wedding coordinator, minister and organist must work through the arrangement of the music selected to begin the service. The organist can offer good suggestions if the bridal couple so desires. In the final moments before the mother of the bride is seated, think of several musical possibilities.

1. A gifted family member quotes Song of Solomon 2:16, "My beloved is mine, and I am his," and sings a song dedicated to the couple.
2. If the bride or groom is gifted musically and if the church is equipped to pre-record the selection, the following reading could be played, followed by special music.

   > **(If the bride is to sing)** "Today marks a new beginning in my life as I give myself to become the wife of (groom's name). The Lord has blessed my life and brought me to this very special moment. As you witness the promises we make and rejoice in the love we share, please remember it is all because of the grace and blessing of the Lord. To my beloved, in a few moments, I will become your wife. My heart is full of love for you. I cherish you and desire to be a godly wife." Special music follows.

   > **(If the groom is to sing)** "Today marks a new beginning in my life as I give myself to become the husband of (bride's name). I cannot begin to describe to you the joy I have in my heart at this moment. The Lord has answered my prayers and brought to me a precious partner in life. As you witness the promises we are about to make, please remember it is all because of the grace and blessing of the Lord. To my beloved, in a few moments, I will become your husband. I cherish you and desire to be a godly husband." Special music follows.

3. Congregational singing can be a fitting way to begin the ceremony. Hymns that speak of the majesty of Christ as well as the Christian home and family create the atmosphere of genuine worship as well as celebration.
4. Occasionally a gifted family member or friend is able to write lyrics to be sung to tunes that are under public domain. This offers a special and creative way to begin the service. It is important to be sure the music is under public domain. Generally, this includes music written before 1922. Various web sites offer public domain titles to be considered.

The lighting of the candles

Many weddings feature the unity candle during the ceremony. Three candles are displayed. Before the ceremony begins, the two outside candles are lit, which represent the bride and groom. Typically the ushers light the candles. Here are several ways to creatively make this special, just before the wedding begins.

1. Both the mother of the bride and the mother of the groom walk together to the unity candles and light the outside candle representing their child.
2. The bride's parents and the groom's parents both come to the unity candle to light the outside candle representing their child. Following the lighting of the candle, a very special moment would occur if both fathers offered prayer for the Lord's blessing upon the new home and family to be established. Or the father of the bride may offer a prayer of thanksgiving for the son-in-law the Lord is bringing into his home and asks the Lord's blessing upon him. The father of the groom likewise offers a prayer of thanksgiving for the daughter-in-law the Lord is bring into his home and asks the Lord's blessing upon

her. The father of the bride then joins the wedding processional to escort his daughter.

3. Another possibility is to involve the grandparents in some way in the lighting of the unity candle. As the candles are being lit, the grandparents stand and someone reads the following. "Today the generations of two homes stand as a tribute and testimony of the faithfulness of God and devotion of families. (Name of groom and name of bride) come together at this moment, to celebrate the amazing plan of God and want you to know they delight in your presence. A new home is established today as another generation embarks on the journey of a lifetime."

Readings

As the two candles at the unity candle display are lit, a precious moment exists to make the ceremony truly unique. A person who has played a special part in the life of either the bride or groom may be invited to share in the wedding ceremony at this point. Consider these special readings.

Special reading—"The Faithfulness of God"

> "We are traveling on a journey along a road of many twists, turns, hills and valleys. This journey of a lifetime begins at the moment of conception when a tiny little person comes into existence as an incredible result of the design of our creator God. These families have witnessed the birth, growth and maturing of two individuals. The bride grew up in (location) and the groom grew up in (location). In a wonderful way, the Lord God has worked in their lives. (At this point, the reader will share how the couple met and one or two specifics as to how the Lord has worked in bringing them together). Now we come to celebrate the faithfulness of God. Jeremiah the prophet declared with assurance in Lamentations 3:22-23, '…His compassions fail not. They are new every morning: great is thy faithfulness.' Truly God is faithful and may His blessing be upon (Name of bride and groom)."

Special reading—"A Parent's Prayer"

This reading can be offered by one of the parents or shared by both the parents of the bride and parents of the groom.

> "Many thoughts go through my mind dear Lord, as I think back on the years I have had with my child. I remember the day we discovered a child would be coming to our home. Thoughts of joy were mixed with the sense of the responsibility of parenting. Then I held this child in my arms. I watched my little one fall asleep as I cradled (name of child) not only in my arms; but close to my heart. I experienced the overwhelming sense of love and awe as well as the desire to protect, and the sheer wonder of being a parent. How amazingly fast the years have flown by! The first steps, the first days of Kindergarten, the first bicycle ride seem like yesterday.
>
> Here we are today. My child will become a life partner, married to another. My family grows in extension today as I welcome into my home

Chapter 8

> and heart the beloved of my child. May the days ahead be filled with love and devotion to you and to each other. May Christ be the head of this new home, and may the wonderful grace and peace of the Lord be part of their lives every day. Lord, may both (name of bride and groom) seek your will, find delight in serving you and know the joy that comes in love that grows. May their love grow deeper as they travel on this journey of a lifetime. I ask this of you dear Lord."

Special reading— "The Journey of Our Lives"

> "Consider the possibility of asking an older individual or couple to write in their own words the blessings experienced in their marriage. This can be a wonderful time when a couple married for many years, very briefly writes of how God has met their needs, blessed their lives and sustained them through the good as well as hard times. This provides a beautiful way for the ceremony to begin."

Special reading—"A Word from the Groom-The Prayer of My Heart"

A creative way to begin the wedding ceremony is to have the groom speak to the congregation immediately after the lighting of the two outside candles at the unity candle display. He may wish to write his own welcome and expression of joy. If he is not a writer, he may wish to read this note entitled, "The Prayer of My Heart."

> "I want to welcome you as family and friends to share in our lives and celebrate our love. (Name of bride) and I want to thank you for coming. I also want you to know that as (bride's name) husband, I sense deeply the responsibility of loving her as Christ loved the church. Before this ceremony begins, as the spiritual leader of our new home, I am asking the Lord to continue to work in our lives. It is the prayer of my heart that Christ would mold me into His image and to help me to become more like Him. It is the prayer of my heart that the Lord would help me to be strong in conviction, gentle in compassion, great in courage and godly in character. May His hand bless our home. May His Word guide our hearts. May His love fill our marriage and help us overcome every obstacle. May His wisdom lead us in each decision. Like Joshua of old, it is the prayer of my heart that as for me and my house, we will serve the Lord.
>
> This is the prayer of my heart for the glory of the Lord Jesus and the good of my beloved (Bride's name). Welcome to our wedding."

Special Features for the Processional

The typical and traditional processional has the bridesmaids, the maid or matron of honor, the ring bearer and flower girl, followed by the father escorting his daughter into the ceremony. As the minister, groom and his groomsmen come into the auditorium, the processional begins and is completed with the father and the bride joining the rest of the party at the front of the church. There are several creative possibilities for the bridal couple to consider.

Groomsmen and bridesmaid meet
Before the arrival of the ring bearer and flower girl, a creative processional has the maids stopping in the aisle at approximately the halfway point. The corresponding groomsman then walks down the aisle, meets the maid, turns and escorts her down the rest of the aisle. The groom also meets his bride in the aisle, shakes hands with the father, escorts his bride to the front with the father of the bride following closely and standing with the couple at the beginning of the ceremony.

Groom and bride only meet in the aisle
Some couples will prefer to have just the bride and groom meet for special escort. The father and bride stop in the aisle and wait for the groom to meet them. Shaking the groom's hand, the father gives his daughter to the groom, who escorts her to the front of the church. The father follows and stands with the wedding party awaiting his speaking part in the service.

Placement of the wedding party in the processional
The typical arrangement of the wedding party places them with their back to the congregation as they face the minister. Usually the wedding party is arranged in the following way.

Back of the Church Auditorium

<u>Ring Bearer</u>   <u>Flower Girl</u>

<u>Groomsmen</u> <u>Best Man</u> <u>Groom</u> <u>Father</u> <u>Bride</u> <u>Maid/Matron</u> <u>Maids</u>

<u>Minister</u>

Front of the Church Auditorium

A special feature that some bridal couples appreciate has the same basic arrangement, except for the direction they face. In this special feature, the bridal party comes to their assigned spot in the front of the church. Following the father of the bride giving his daughter to be married, the bridal party will turn toward the congregation. As the entire party faces the assembled guests, the minister takes his place in the front center, facing the bridal party with his back to the congregation.

Special Features for the Wedding Ceremony
The possibilities are nearly unlimited in creating a unique and special ceremony. Typical special features include special music, Scripture readings and the lighting of the unity candle from the two outside candles. You as the officiating pastor may wish to offer some of the additional special features that can be placed in the wedding ceremony. The following are several ideas that may be considered.

Special honor to the parents of the bride and groom
Some bridal couples wish to honor their parents in the wedding ceremony by presenting a special gift. The bride gives the gift to her parents as the groom gives a gift to his parents.

Typically the parents are not told about this so as to be surprised in the service. A variation of this act would be to reverse the giving of the gifts. Here the bride would come to her husband's parents and the groom to his bride's parents. This is a tender expression of love and appreciation to the parents.

Special tribute to the Lord for His wonderful leading
This tribute provides a tender moment in the service and makes it truly unique to the couple. The officiating pastor with the help of the bridal couple fills in the blanks and reads the following tribute.

> Proverbs 3:5-6 says, "Trust in the Lord with all thine heart, and lean not unto thine own understanding. In all thy ways acknowledge him, and he shall direct thy paths." Today, we as family and friends gather to recognize and celebrate the incredible way the Lord has directed the paths of (name of groom) and (name of bride).
>
> (Groom) was born in (name of town and state). As child he grew up in (name of town and state). He placed his trust in the Lord Jesus as Savior at the age of (age). God tenderly worked in his life. (Bride) was born in (name of town and state). As a child she grew up in (name of town and state). She placed her trust in the Lord Jesus as Savior at the age of (age). God tenderly worked in her life.
>
> "And He shall direct thy paths," so says the Lord. In a special way, the Lord has directed in the lives of (groom) and (bride). They met (testimony of how they met and how the Lord has directed them to this day. This may include a humorous event, special direction in their lives, or whatever their testimony might be.)
>
> We as their family and friends give thanks to the Lord for the way He has directed their paths. There is no improvement on the will of God. Though the road will not be easy, great is the joy of knowing the Lord's direction and trusting Him for the days ahead.

Special charge to the couple
The officiating pastor or invited special guest may share the following charge to the couple. This is a great opportunity to invest both in the couple to be married as well as in the marriages of the invited guests.

> Today marks the day of a new beginning. We gather here as your family and friends to share the joy of this moment and to witness the sacred vows you share today. The uniting of your lives and the establishing of your new home is special not only to us; but is special to the Lord Himself. It is my privilege to present to you a solemn but also joyful charge. A charge is that by which one is reminded and entrusted with

the sacred responsibility assigned to him or her. (Groom) and (Bride), as you stand before the Lord and these witnesses, I charge you today to honor the Lord your God in all your ways.

(Groom), as the head of this new home and the spiritual leader of your family, I charge you to love your wife as Christ loved His church. I charge you to be a devoted, faithful, loving, protecting, and godly husband. I charge you to keep yourself from any temptation that would hurt your marriage. May the enabling of the Lord and the empowering of His Word be yours every day.

(Bride), as the partner and wife of (groom), I charge you to follow the Lord your God and be all He wants you to be. I charge you to encourage your husband. Be a devoted, faithful, loving, and godly wife. I charge you to be gracious in your actions and devoted in your commitment to your husband. I charge you to be a woman of prayer and godly character. I charge you to keep yourself from any temptation that would hurt your marriage. May God enable you to follow Him every day.

Special reading—"When Two People Really Love"

We read of Isaac's love for Rebekah his bride. Genesis 24:67 states, "And Isaac brought her into his mother's tent, and took Rebekah, and she became his wife; and he loved her..." Isaac grew up in a home that honored the Lord. He saw the Lord's blessing upon his parents and their walk with God. But something was missing in his life. In a wonderful way, the Lord incredibly brought to him Rebekah, his beloved. And he loved her.

When two people come together at the leading of the Lord, a wonderful relationship of love is established. This love grows deep as it is centered in the Lord. When two people really love each other, they will discover encouragement even in discouraging days. They will receive grace in times that are stressful. They will find forgiveness in the moments when misunderstandings happen. When two people really love each other, there is no obstacle too big to overcome. There is no trial too hard to endure. There is no hardship too heavy to bear.

When two people really love each other, a home of godliness is established. A closeness of fellowship is experienced and an intimacy is realized that is more precious than all the gold of the mines, and more valuable than all the wealth of Wall Street. When two people really love each other, it truly is as long as life shall last. This love comes from the One Who loves you both more than anyone else could ever love you. This love that lasts a lifetime is from the Lord Jesus, who loves you with all of His heart.

Special Scripture passages

A wedding ceremony offers a special opportunity for planting seeds in the lives of the family and friends invited. Couples may wish to have Scripture inserted in their ceremony. Among the many passages of Scripture that could be used, here is a partial list of possibilities.

- Genesis 2:18-25
- Genesis 24:61-67
- Psalm 8
- Psalm 16:5-11
- Psalm 33:1-5
- Psalm 100
- Psalm 127
- Psalm 128
- 1 Corinthians 13
- Ephesians 5:21-33
- Colossians 1:9-18
- Titus 2:1-8, 11-13
- 1 Peter 3:1-12

Special presentation of the bride and groom

Traditionally the father of the bride is asked, "Who gives this woman to be married to this man?" He usually answers, "Her mother and I do."

As a special feature that makes the wedding ceremony unique is the creative way the couple is given and presented to each other. In this feature, when asked, "Who gives this woman to be married to this man?" The mother of the bride joins the wedding party and states with her husband, **"We joyfully give our daughter."** (Mother and father of the bride then kiss daughter, shake the hand of the groom or hug him and are seated.) The minister then asks, "Who gives this man to be married to this woman?" His parents come and take their place with the groom and states, **"We joyfully give our son."** (His parents then hug him and hug the bride as well.)

The officiating pastor then says, "How beautifully from two different families, one new family forms today. As parents, your greatest joy comes from seeing your children walk in truth. May the home established today be a home of joy and truth built upon the solid foundation of Christ."

Special reading—"A Parent's Prayer"

This reading could be read by either set of parents or a parent from both sets.

> Lord, today is an amazing day. It is a day that I imagined long ago and it has arrived much faster than I ever dreamed. Lord, our children come before You today to share their joy and promise each other their lives.
>
> Lord, as this day has come, we the parents of (groom) and (bride) are filled with wonder and awe at Your precious leading. I pray for our children today. I pray for their home that it will be a shining tribute of You and Your grace. I pray for their marriage. May it be a union that is marked by kindness, forgiveness, joy, and love. I pray today that their joy would be full and their blessings many.
>
> Lord, I do not pray that You would make them rich. I pray that You would supply their need. Lord, I do not pray You would make the way easy. I pray that You would direct their steps. Lord, I do not pray You

> would make them famous. I pray that You would give them good friends that would encourage and enrich them with a friendship centered in You. Lord, today has come and with it our heartfelt thanks, as parents who love You and pray the very best for our children.

Special reading—"A Marriage Built On Christ"

Wise couples trust the Lord and daily understand

We're here by His good leading and secure in His precious hand.

Together we enter our marriage. I will love you all of my life.

May this sacred union be blessed, as a godly husband and wife.

We truly need the Lord's blessing in all we say and do.

By His grace and help each day my love, I promise to be true.

The words of our vows, our covenant will last throughout our life.

I rejoice in this special moment when we become husband and wife.

Before this assembly we promise, to follow the Lord every day.

May He give power and blessing and guard the words we say.

May we quickly be forgiving when those hurts surely come.

May our home be Christ-like always, and our hearts to Him belong.

Dismissal of the Wedding Guests

Traditionally, the bridal party participates in the recessional following the presentation and introduction of the new married couple. The wedding party assembles in a line in the foyer as the designated groomsman returns to escort the bride's parents first and then the second groomsman escorts the groom's parents to the receiving line. Two groomsmen return to dismiss the assembly row by row beginning with the bride's side.

Some bridal couples prefer to dismiss the congregation personally by returning to the front of the auditorium. Together they dismiss row by row, briefly greeting family and friends in the aisle. This provides a precious moment to share the joy and dismiss the assembly often more quickly. Guests are not as apt to stand and speak at length in the aisle in front of other guests as they will in the foyer! It is a nice way to greet and proceed to pictures and the reception.

The possibilities are nearly unlimited in creating and fashioning a truly unique and biblical wedding. May the Lord bless you as the officiating pastor as you oversee the celebration and shepherd this couple through their wedding. You have invested countless hours in their lives. The premarital counseling is time well worth the investment. As a new home is being established, your work has prepared the way for generations.

Chapter Nine—The Reception

A Time of Celebration

By the time the wedding ceremony is completed and the last of the pictures are taken, many pastors breathe a sigh of relief and look forward to the reception. Other than perhaps praying for the refreshments, typically the pastor has no further responsibility and enjoys being with others to celebrate the couple's joy.

Regarding the reception, there may be a few things you as the officiating pastor might wish to help the couple think through. In what counseling session do you speak to them about the reception? What are your standards for marrying couples and what is allowed or discouraged and forbidden in the reception? Are there different standards to which you hold if the reception is held at church rather than off the church campus?

This is an outstanding opportunity to help the couple understand that the reception is the first official act in their new married lives. As believers, we are to live new, Christ-changed lives (2 Corinthians 5:17). The wedding reception of two redeemed people who love the Lord Jesus should be very different from the reception of two unsaved people who are of the world.

The wedding reception of the believing couple provides a special opportunity for fun and fellowship. Precious opportunities to make a truly creative and unique reception are available to couples. Work through the answers to some important questions.

1. Does our reception glorify the Lord Jesus and give Him a pre-eminent place?
2. Does our reception abstain from anything that is of the world and contrary to sound doctrine?
3. Does our reception clearly present the blessing and joy of a biblical home and family to those attending?
4. Does our reception celebrate the goodness of the Lord in bringing us as a couple together?
5. Does our reception establish the permanence of pledging our love for our life time as a couple?
6. Does our reception create a day that will bring memories of joy through out the years to come?
7. Does our reception provide opportunity for the families to clearly see the establishment of a new home and biblical family?
8. Does our reception focus on the establishment of marriage as being God's plan and His idea?
9. Does our reception enhance and elevate the marriage of believers and the joy which comes from the Lord?

> Permission is granted to reproduce these guidelines for both the church as well as the couple. Many pastors would not marry any couple if alcoholic beverages were to be served at the reception. May the Lord give you wisdom in establishing your guidelines.

Creative Ideas for Godly Receptions

Make the reception of the believing couple truly different. Here are several suggestions to consider.

Forget a modified "Christian" toast

Raising glasses and pretending the sparkling grape juice is champagne should be meaningless to a godly believer. Rather, bring both sets of parents as well as the bride and groom for a special presentation and prayer. Consider having the groom's parents stand beside the bride and the bride's parents stand beside the groom. A special prayer asking the Lord to bless the couple is a great testimony.

A brief statement of testimony

The best man and/or the matron or maid of honor sharing a testimony would be a great memory maker for the guests. This could be a time of sharing how the Lord brought the bride and groom together, or it could be a time of sharing how God has blessed their individual lives through the friendship of the bride and groom. It may also include a testimony of how the bride and groom came to personal faith in the Lord Jesus Christ.

Special readings

Any of the readings offered in the wedding ceremony could easily be incorporated into the reception activities.

Brief Power Point presentation

If given enough time to prepare, a wonderful possibility exists in the production of a Power Point presentation of the bride and groom. This would include photos from infancy up to the present. A note of caution would concern the length of the presentation. Neither the bride nor groom will desire a lengthy slide show!

Special music

As in the wedding ceremony, special music in the reception can be a huge blessing. Other couples may enjoy quiet music in the background during the time of eating at the reception.

Gifts

Many couples appreciate the opportunity of returning home to a much smaller circle of family to open the gifts. If this is possible, often it is much more enjoyable. Several should be asked ahead of time to collect the gifts. These should be stored at the home of trusted family or friends, not in the empty apartment of the honeymooning couple.

While this volume does not address the honeymoon, excellent resources are available for the couple to read and use. See Chapter Six for several suggestions.

Chapter Ten— Suggested Timeline

Countdown to the Wedding

With the abundance of wedding planners available today, surely the bride has ample suggestions as to when the events of the wedding ceremony should be scheduled. It is important to remember that wedding planners are only suggestions. There will be occasions when the bridal couple will ask you for suggested dates to complete the plans for the ceremony. For those couples not using a formal wedding planner, below is a suggested time line you may share with them for basic wedding schedules. It is written to the couple.

Once you are engaged:
1. Begin to think through the wedding budget. This will determine the size and style of the wedding. Talk with the parents of the bride and decide who will pay for specific details of the wedding. The next chapter will offer a suggestion as to who pays for the various items of the wedding and reception. Determine that the Lord will be glorified throughout the wedding and the reception. This is a time to glorify Him and not glamorize selves.
2. Select a wedding date and time. Speak with your pastor and book the church and fellowship hall for the reception.
3. Will you be using a wedding coordinator? Work with your pastor in the selection of the wedding coordinator as well as the exact expectations you have concerning her role.
4. Ask the pastor his procedure and dates for premarital counseling. Assure him you are eager to prepare for your marriage. Determine to be on guard and not allow temptation to cause you to experience moral impurity.
5. Register at local bridal registries. Target, Wal-Mart, Bed Bath and Beyond and JC Penny are but a few of such stores.
6. Select and retain the photographer. Be sure to compare prices and ask what the photographer offers in the package. Wise stewardship really demands careful selection of each venue of your wedding and reception.

Six months before the wedding ceremony:
1. Begin to compile the guest list. A great source for the various family members and friends will come from both the mothers and grandmothers of the bride and groom. What about the church family? Begin to discuss how they will be invited. Will a general announcement of invitation be made with a sign-up sheet? Or will individuals within the church family receive a specific invitation?

2. Select and order the wedding gown. Make sure there is plenty of time for it to arrive and any alterations to take place. This is a special day for the bride. However, as a godly believer, she must be sure the gown passes the following tests.
    - <u>The modesty test</u>-is anything showing that should not be?
    - <u>The stewardship test</u>-while this gown is for a very special occasion, the average length of time a bride wears her gown is less than four hours. Is the amount of money this specific bridal gown costs a wise investment? When a four-hour gown costs the same as four months rent, is this really wise?
    - <u>The comfort test</u>-is this comfortable and will the bride enjoy being in this for the hours of the ceremony, pictures and reception?
3. Double-check with the pastor as to when he wishes to begin premarital counseling. Probably at this point, the pastor will wish to schedule your first appointment. Do not be surprised if he has several pages of information for you to fill out and submit before your first appointment.
4. Work with your wedding coordinator in retaining the services of the organist, janitor, videographer, and florist. Be sure to double-check with the photographer to make sure the date is still confirmed.
5. Some bridal couples send out a "Be sure to save the date card" for our wedding.
6. Choose the wedding rings.
7. Send the engagement announcements to the newspapers.
8. Select the attendants (bridesmaids and groomsmen). These should be people who are either related to the bridal couple or are really significant in the friendship. In a truly godly wedding, the attendants should be like-minded believers who are walking with the Lord.
9. Select the wedding cake. Wise shopping will really pay off in the cake selection. Will the cake come from a professional bakery, or will it be made by a friend or acquaintance?
10. Complete the honeymoon plans. If you are traveling outside the country, check on visa, passports and any required inoculations.
11. Check on the availability and prices of salons if the bride and her maids will require their services.
12. Book the caterer and enter the contractual agreement to reserve the date. This can only be completed after the couple decides what kind of reception they will have. Will it be a cake and punch reception? Will it be a sit-down catered meal? Who will be paying for it? What is affordable?
13. Check with area motels. If it is possible to hold a block of rooms without penalty for cancellation, it will be wise to do so.

Four months before the wedding ceremony:
1. Confirm the date and final details with the caterer. A written contract should be signed by both the caterer and the person who is paying for the reception.
2. Order and purchase items not being furnished by the caterer for the reception and ceremony. Wedding receptions are negotiable as to what the caterer will

include in the price. Decide carefully what the family will furnish and what will be part of the caterer's price.
3. Order the wedding invitations.
4. Visit with the photographer to work out specific details of the wedding and reception.
5. Check with the florist to confirm your wishes for the flowers. You will most likely have to at least make a partial payment, if not pay in full at this time.
6. Begin to gather estimates for the decorations for the reception.
7. Purchase the wedding rings.
8. Order tuxedos for the groomsmen and the fathers.
9. Check with the local city or village clerk as to marriage license requirements.

Two months before the wedding ceremony:
1. Meet with your wedding coordinator to review details and deadlines for the wedding and reception.
2. Mail invitations to the invited guests. This is usually done between six weeks and two months before the wedding.
3. Finalize arrangements for out-of-town attendants and guests. Where will they stay? By this time, there are so many details to work through, it is often much easier for out-of-town guests to be furnished the name of the motel or motels available, along with the telephone numbers. Make it clear that the bridal couple and families would really appreciate family and friends booking their own rooms.
4. Select a small but meaningful gift for the attendants and those helping with the wedding.
5. Check with the Social Security Administration concerning the bride's name change and her social security number.
6. You will be scheduling regular counseling appointments with the pastor. Commit to taking seriously the tests, assignments and counsel provided by your pastor. He has invested much time and prayer in your premarital counseling. Demonstrate your appreciation to him.

One month before the wedding ceremony:
1. Meet regularly with the wedding coordinator. Check, double-check, and review the details on the wedding coordinator's list.
2. Double check with all vendors to make sure the date is confirmed.
3. Have final fitting for bridal party.
4. Have groomsmen fitted for tuxedos.
5. Check with newspaper on wedding announcement requirements.
6. Finalize plans with the pastor as well as finalize plans for the rehearsal dinner.

These are suggested dates and goals. If the bridal party you are working with tends to procrastinate, it may be wise to encourage them to set firm deadlines for these important activities. It is wise to consider this as part of the premarital counseling process. Being timely in the wedding plans will help to remove some tension and pressure as the wedding date approaches. Such timeliness will also help you as the pastor to assess the maturity of the couple as well as provide a glimpse into their future handling of responsibilities.

Chapter Eleven—Financial Guidelines

Who Pays for What in the Wedding and Reception?

How do we know who usually pays for the various items in the wedding and reception? There are no set and absolutely hard-and-fast rules for who pays for what in the upcoming ceremony. Several circumstances contribute to the question of funding. Is the couple employed with adequate salaries, and will they have a significant part in paying for the wedding or reception? On the other hand, will the parents of the bride be paying significantly for this wonderful event?

While there are no absolutes, typically the following individuals pay for these various items in the wedding ceremony:

The bride typically pays for the following:
- The wedding ring for the groom
- Gifts for her attendants
- A small gift for her husband (if they choose to give each other a gift)
- A bridesmaid's luncheon (if one is planned)
- Wedding night lingerie and items to be taken on the honeymoon

The groom typically pays for the following:
- The wedding ring for the bride
- Honeymoon vacation
- Wedding gift for the bride (if they choose to give each other a gift)
- Gifts for the groomsmen
- Pastor's honorarium

The bride's family typically pays for the following:
- The wedding ceremony costs
- The bride's attire
- The wedding invitations, announcements, thank you notes
- The wedding photographer
- The wedding organist and church janitor
- The florist
- The reception
- Note: Many parents find it helpful and encouraging to give the bridal couple a set amount of money to be used for the wedding ceremony and reception. Whatever the couple does not use is theirs for whatever expenses they have (rent, etc.)

The groom's family typically pays for the following:
- Their attire and the rehearsal dinner

The attendants typically pay for the following:
- The attire to be worn in the wedding
- Gifts to be given to the newlyweds
- Their own transportation to and from the wedding

Chapter Twelve—The Postwedding Follow-Up Counseling Session

The Couple and Their Adjustments Six Months Later

During the premarital phase it was mandatory that the couple be faithful in keeping their appointments and completing their homework. It may be interesting to see the difference in couples as to their level of commitment and diligence in their efforts to prepare for marriage.

Now that the couple is married, you as the officiating pastor do not have the same leverage in their lives. Before, if they didn't come for the appointment or if they didn't do the homework, you would not marry them. Today they are already married. Postmarital follow-up can only be offered.

Some pastors prefer offering a two-month postwedding follow-up. Others prefer a six month session. Either is fine. In fact, some may wish to incorporate both possibilities. This material is written for the six-month follow-up. You are welcome to make adjustments and set the follow-up at your preference.

Assuming there are no emergency counseling appointments soon after the wedding, the follow-up session at six months is designed to assess the level of resolution of conflicts and to detect areas in the adjustment process that should be addressed. The test material "Now That We Are Married" (found in their couple's edition) should be assigned early enough that it is copied and turned in at least two weeks before their postwedding counseling session. Also use the answers of Section 10 of "The Road Already Traveled." Compare how they answered before their wedding with how they view the questions now.

Now That We Are Married

My name: _____

List three things for which you are thankful in your marriage: _____

_____

_____

List three things you appreciate about your mate: _____

_____

_____

Use a scale of 1 to 5 to answer the following questions:
- 1= Very dissatisfied and very concerned, needs immediate attention
- 2= Dissatisfied and concerned, we need to work on this
- 3= All right, but surely could improve
- 4= Satisfied with this situation and appreciate this blessing
- 5= Very satisfied and thank the Lord for this and will not take it for granted

Mark the appropriate number by circling it for your answer. Place an X over the number you believe will be your partner's level of satisfaction. Please do not work on this together. Work separately and prayerfully on your answers.

1. The state of our walk with the Lord as a couple
   1 2 3 4 5

2. The routine we are developing in reading the Bible and praying together
   1 2 3 4 5

3. Our involvement in our local church   1 2 3 4 5

4. The daily time invested in talking with each other   1 2 3 4 5

5. The quality of free time we have to spend with each on a regular basis
   1 2 3 4 5

6. The amount of time we are apart from each other because of work and other activities   1 2 3 4 5

7. The way we are managing our money   1 2 3 4 5

8. The way we are adjusting to each other   1 2 3 4 5

9. The way we are making decisions together   1 2 3 4 5

10. The way we are managing conflicts when differing opinions surface   1 2 3 4 5

11. Our sexual interaction with each other   1 2 3 4 5

12. Our level of involvement with friends and doing things with other couples   1 2 3 4 5

13. My spouse's relationship with my parents   1 2 3 4 5

14. My relationship with my spouse's parents   1 2 3 4 5

15. The level of satisfaction with our marriage   1 2 3 4 5

What are some of the situations you wish to discuss with the pastor? _____

_____

_____

> Those two very good illustrations of the bank and the lawn really apply now. To have a healthy bank account, more deposits must be made than withdrawals. To have a healthy marriage, make far more investments than withdrawals. To have a healthy lawn, it takes work and care. The same is true with a healthy marriage.

The Road Already Traveled- Section 10

Section 10. Complete the following statements in your own words.

A. When I think about marriage, I feel- _____

B. Some of the things I appreciate about my future mate include- _____

C. Among my expectations in marriage, several that are very important to me include- _____

D. Several areas that need to improve in my life would include- _____

Several areas that need to improve in the life of my future mate would include- _____

E. When I think of the number of children I would like to have it would be- _____

F. When I think of the ideal way of spending an evening together with my mate, it would be- _____

G. When I think of the ideal vacation, it would be- _____

88 *From This Day Forward*

Begin the Session

Start the session with a personal illustration of some of the adjustments (without going into too much detail and taking too much time) of your own marriage. Share with the couple the blessings you have today because you and your wife were and are still committed to each other as well as investing in your marriage to make it work.

How very important it is to remind the couple that they are in a critically important time in their marriage. The first year together will be a key to the rest of their lives. Adjustments will be many. It is not uncommon to discover several disappointments after the wedding ceremony. The couple may be quite surprised at how much they did not really know about each other until they were married.

Some of the couples will still be in the "honeymoon stage" if you choose to meet with them before the two-month marker. Routines of schedules, daily duties and the running of the household are just beginning to settle in. By the six-month marker, patterns of habit, lifestyle, and personality issues are clearly surfacing. This session provides the pastor a great opportunity to reassure them that all couples have adjustments to make. It is when situations are not addressed and corrected that marriages begin to suffer at this point.

As the counseling pastor, you have noted the answers provided on the returned test papers. The circle around the number is the answer of the person filling out the answer sheet. The X on the number indicates how the person responding believes his or her spouse will answer. The design of this test will help you to identify how the couple is progressing in their understanding of each other as well as how the adjustments are coming along.

As you counsel through the test answers, the purpose of the session is to bring the couple to several places of ongoing commitment.

Commitment to invest generously in my marriage

Matthew 6:19-21 admonishes us to avoid being focused on treasure that is only "here and now" in nature. Rather, be rich in laying up treasure in Heaven. This means to keep spiritual and eternal things as your priority. The Lord Jesus makes personal the application by saying, "For where your treasure is, there will your heart be also" (verse 21). Are the hearts of the couple truly focused on the spiritual aspects of a successful marriage? Do they demonstrate that they have wholeheartedly committed to working on the growth and maturity of their relationship?

Investment in marriage requires time, talking and truthfulness with self and each other. As you assess their answers, is there clear evidence of growth in their relationship? Are they really putting their hearts into this relationship?

Is the couple committed to being sensitive and understanding with each other? Paul's writing to the Colossian believers in 3:12-13 provides a list of characteristics the Lord desires to grow and display in every believer, regardless of temperament and personality. Understanding the meaning of these concepts will enrich their marriage.

1. <u>Bowels of mercies</u> (12a) has to do with a heart of compassion. It is the opposite of being harsh, cruel, mean-spirited, or obnoxious. This heart of compassion should overflow with care for the other person.
2. <u>Kindness</u> (12b) is a thoughtful demonstration toward the other, a sweetness of attitude and action. This will be seen in the details of sharing household chores, encouraging each other, and the quality of time spent together.
3. <u>Humbleness of mind and meekness</u> (12c) does not act as a doormat willing to be walked all over by another individual. Rather, it is gentleness and graciousness extended to others. It is the opposite of being arrogant and haughty.
4. <u>Longsuffering</u> (12d) will be expressed with patience even if I have been provoked. It is the opposite of being short-fused and explosive when things do not go the way I wish. Steadfastness and perseverance are both essential elements of longsuffering.
5. <u>Forbearing one another</u> (13a) is much more than just putting up with people. This concept expressed by Paul to the Colossian believers demonstrates sustaining, enduring, and bearing with people. It extends grace where grace is not merited. Truth is communicated with carefulness and loving tenderness. When there is a disagreement, confrontation is not explosive but quiet and timely.
6. <u>Forgiving one another</u> (13b) cancels the debt of the offender. It is the response of the wounded party when the guilty apologizes and asks to be forgiven. Genuine forgiveness does not keep a score card of wounds to bring up later. Forgiveness is granted on the basis of how Christ has freely forgiven us.

These essential elements are the consistent and typical actions of a marriage that is adjusting well to each other and working through areas of potential conflict. From the answers on the homework as well as the demeanor of the couple in the counseling center, do you see that these characteristics are being consistently applied?

Commitment to guard against the serious dangers that harm a home and marriage

The writer of Hebrews points out three serious roots of sin from which a wide variety of sinful actions will grow. From these three roots, sins of omission as well as sins of commission originate.

1. <u>Root of bitterness</u> (Hebrews 12:15a). This bitterness is an anger and resentment simmering just below the surface. While everyone experiences times of anger, this is beyond the typical. This is an angry person, who allows bitterness to grow and fester.

    Several of the outflows of the angry person include seeking revenge, wrath, loss of temper, slamming doors, screaming, words of venom, a mean spirit as well as grumbling and complaining about how unfair things are. Anger is like a cancerous growth that, if left untreated, not only destroys healthy bodies, but it brings about devastation in relationships.

    Are obvious areas of resentment and anger displayed from either the tests or the attitudes of the couple? Gentle probing may be required to scratch the surface in reaching the bitterness. Do not automatically accept the "We are fine, pastor. No problems to work on" answer given by many couples. Listen carefully to their answers and watch intently their non-verbal communication of facial gestures and posturing.

2. <u>Fornication</u> (12:16a). From this word, *pornos,* comes the wide range of illicit and sinful sexual activities. God has created a beautiful expression of intense intimacy for the husband and wife in the warmth of emotional intimacy and the act of sexual intercourse. The enemy of home and marriage has defiled this expression with sordid temptation and opportunity to lust. Pornography and unfaithfulness are great enemies of the home and family.

    Counseling in the realm of sexual matters is frequently uncomfortable for both the couple as well as the pastor. However, a healthy sexual relationship and growth in emotional intimacy are very important elements in a healthy marriage. Sex and intimacy are two different but necessary things. Both are necessary for a healthy marriage. What areas of protection are built into the marriage relating to internet filters? How much quality free time does the couple have on a weekly basis? Are there specific areas through which the couple must be counseled regarding moral purity?

3. <u>Profane living</u> (12:16b). Here the idea of profanity is presented in the words that are communicated and a lifestyle that is lived. Literally this profanity pictures a person coming to the threshold of the door and being denied entrance because of a violation or making common what God says is holy. It is demonstrated by wrong values, self-focus, and wrong priorities. The attitudes of self-gratification (I want it now), self-indulgence (I have a right to be happy) and self-interest (I am the most important person in the whole wide world) express themselves through attitudes and choices of the heart.

    Wrong values, jealousy, covetousness, poor money management, worldly living and dishonesty are several of the ways this enemy of the home is manifested. One of the most dangerous situations a newly established home faces is indebtedness to accumulate possessions. Unwise couples insist upon having things right now that took many years of working and saving for their parents to acquire. Indebtedness is a web woven that is difficult to break through.

The post-wedding follow-up counseling session will address these areas based upon the counseling needs of the couple. This will be time well invested as this couple begins their lifetime together.

Conclude the Session

Direct the couple to the worksheet (next chapter) entitled, "Fifteen Ways to Build a Strong Marriage." Briefly review these things, making suggestions and comments to further illustrate the importance of building their lives upon the Lord and His Word.

Chapter Thirteen

Supplemental Worksheets and Additional Counseling Aids

Throughout the premarital counseling program, various situations will arise that will require additional attention and work. The following materials are from various marriage workshops presented by the author. Permission is granted to copy these and use them in any of your counseling programs.

The first material presented, *"Fifteen Ways to Build a Strong Marriage,"* is to be used with the six-month postwedding counseling session. You are welcome to use this in earlier sessions if so desired.

"The Top Ten Wise Things Smart Couples Still Do" is designed to encourage couples to invest in each other's lives in wise ways. Live each day to the fullest potential blessing and seek to become the help meet God intends for you to be. These ten things are actual statements made to the author by couples across America. Some of the couples have been married many years. Their counsel is wise, and applying it will be helpful to each couple.

"The Top Ten Blessings of a Great Marriage" provides ten practical goals for every couple to keep in view. These ten situations may be obvious to some couples. However, there is a huge difference between knowing and doing (John 13:17).

"Help For Those Who Grew Up in a Troubled Home" is a resource counseling agenda for individuals who are struggling because of an unhappy past. Overcoming past hurts without bringing them into the marriage is crucial. For those who grew up in an unhappy home, there is help.

> Permission is given to add personal notes and questions to these supplemental aids. Depending on the severity of the situation, several additional counseling sessions may be needed.

Fifteen Ways to Build a Strong Marriage

Marriages, in some ways, are similar to building a house. Both must be built on strong foundations, directions must be followed, and careful attention to details must be given. Developing a daily consistency in the following areas will help you to build a strong marriage. It is well worth the time and investment.

1. Be sure you and your mate are becoming best friends.
2. Develop good conversational skills. Do not interrupt. Look at each other. Speak clearly without sarcasm or hurtful words.
3. Share openly with each other about your fears, concerns and what you are thinking.

4. Learn to be considerate of your mate's feelings.
5. Develop the skill to become better aware of the little details of life and the home, which will demonstrate thoughtfulness to your mate.
6. Avoid developing a critical spirit. Do not criticize your mate. When you must address a situation, express it carefully, prayerfully and tenderly.
7. Frequently tell your mate of your love.
8. Become good in demonstrating that you are not taking your mate for granted.
9. Never be in competition with your mate.
10. Discover God's purpose for your life.
11. Determine to grow as a Christian.
12. Find ways to serve the Lord together.
13. Ask the Lord to help you to reach an agreement concerning earning, saving, investing, spending and sharing your money.
14. Respect your mate.
15. Work at having a great relationship with the extended family. However always remember, your first priority is the Lord and next your mate.

"Together-What a Beautiful Word"

Together we've walked with the Lord hand in hand,

Our marriage is built on the rock, not sifting sand.

It has sometimes been hard, but always we've known,

Always be careful. We will reap what we've sown.

So we've sown kindness and joy, and of course lots of love.

Our blessings are many, He has showered from above.

We're convinced as we travel, God's will is the best,

Seek Him first and we'll find, He'll supply all the rest.

Matthew 6:33, "Seek ye first the kingdom of God, and His righteousness; and all these things shall be added unto you."

The Top Ten Wise Things Smart Couples Still Do

Great marriages do not just happen. Saying "I do" on your wedding day, with little or no investment and involvement in your marriage, is not a guarantee of a happy and growing relationship. Those couples who stay happily married for decades all seem to have a common thread interwoven throughout their marriage. In addition to trusting the Lord Jesus for salvation, these couples identify and consistently implement ten important things in their lives.

10. **Talk to each other graciously**-Proverbs 10:11, 19-20, 32. They understand the words and tone of voice can help or hurt their partner.

9. **Seek God's will earnestly**-Psalm 143:10. There is no greater joy than doing the plan God shows a couple, in the place God leads the couple, with the

people God entrusts to the couple, through the power the Lord gives to the couple.

8. **Treat each other thoughtfully**-Matthew 19:5-6. The tender and thoughtful courtesies extended to each other throughout the dating process continue on and grow far beyond the marriage ceremony. Every day provides opportunity to demonstrate consideration and kindness to each other. A thoughtful action greatly assists the one-flesh unity of which the Lord speaks. Acts that are thoughtless and unkind push people apart and the one-flesh unity suffers.

7. **Forgive those hurts quickly**-Ephesians 4:30-32. No marriage is perfect. Every couple has plenty of opportunities for forgiveness to be needed and extended.

6. **Cast their cares on the Lord completely**-1 Peter 5:7. Throughout the lifetime of marriage, a wide variety of experiences will surely take place. Some of the greatest joys and blessings will come. And some of the greatest heartaches and disappointments will likewise be experienced. In the hard times, couples will be blessed as they quietly and deliberately cast their cares upon the Lord.

    Couples who pray together, embrace each other and cherish each other in the hard times will find a great source of strength in the trial as they apply this great Biblical principle.

5. **Model their roles biblically**-Ephesians 5:21-33. What a vivid object lesson the Lord displays in the lives of the husband and wife! The role of the husband is to biblically model the life of love, devotion, and commitment of Christ to the church. Holding nothing back that is helpful, the devoted husband lives for his wife and gives her a place held by no other person.

    Likewise, the love, devotion and respect that the church renders to the Lord is modeled in a beautiful way in the life of the godly wife. The submission spoken of in the text is not that of fear and burden. It is the respect and loyalty of a godly wife who looks to her husband for leadership, protection and wisdom.

4. **View their children thankfully**-Psalm 127-128. In the timing and plan of the Lord, children are a wonderful blessing. While sometimes a great challenge, ultimately children are a joy. Wise couples often tell their children how thankful they are that God has brought them into their lives.

3. **Affirm their devotion tenderly**-Proverbs 5:15-20. The writer of Proverbs is very frank and forthcoming about the joy of one husband and one wife finding sexual thrill and satisfaction exclusively within their marriage relationship. The tender affirmation of the husband and wife is not limited to the sexual act of marriage, but also in the words and deeds of daily living.

2. **Serve the Lord together gladly**-Psalm 100:2. Wise couples are not only members of the local church; they are faithful, active, and find opportunities to serve the Lord.

1. **Love each other totally**- Song of Solomon 2:16. They belong to each other. Instead of the words "me" and "I", the common expression has become "we" and "us" in daily living. This is the agape love that is a decision of the will, seeking the well being and best interests of the other, even when it is not deserved. Such love holds back anything that is hurtful, rude, arrogant or self-serving. The wise couple, knowing their marriage is for a lifetime, daily seeks opportunity to not only love each other; but discovers ways to express it to each other.

The Top Ten Blessings of a Great Marriage

Only in horseshoes does coming close count. There are no substitutes for a happy and healthy marriage. Do not settle for a marriage that is less than great. The Lord Jesus desires to work in precious ways throughout the lifetime of the couple. As they trust Him, learn of His ways, apply His Word, and grow in their personal walk with Him, a great marriage can take place. The blessings of such a marriage are reflected in the following blessings:

1. **A great friendship**-Song of Solomon 2:4. "His banner over me was love." The bride of Solomon was delighted that the love of her life was also her very best friend.

2. **A great example**-1 Corinthians 11:1. "Be ye followers of me, even as I also am of Christ" is not the statement of arrogance. It is rather the honest, quiet expression of surrender to the Lord and consistent living of His principles. Though the couple may not say it in words, others will be able to see the results of a great marriage and say, "I want my marriage to be like theirs."

3. **A great prayer support**-1 Peter 3:7. A dishonored marriage relationship results in a hindered prayer life. What an incredible connection takes place when the husband and wife are prayer partners! What a wonderful blessing in the life of a great marriage!

4. **A great opportunity to demonstrate a servant's spirit**-Romans 6:22. Writing to the church at Rome, Paul reminded these early believers that they were freed from being slaves to sin. Now they would discover the joy of being servants of the Lord with fruitful and holy living unto Him. Great marriages are not harsh, demanding and self-centered. When husband and wife overcome the temptation to be arrogant, thoughtless and hard to live with, a beautiful desire to live for each other grows into genuine service.

5. **A great illustration is possible**-Ephesians 5:21-33. The illustration of Christ and His church is demonstrated beautifully by a godly husband and his wife. Love, protection, and devotion evidenced in the life of the husband, as well as respect, submission, and appreciation modeled by the godly wife combine to beautifully illustrate the spiritual reality of Christ and the church.

6. **A great security is enjoyed**-Proverbs 24:3. Trust is a wonderful thing. It takes time to grow and develop. Unfortunately, it can be damaged or ruined

very quickly. The security of a marriage and home being built by wisdom and understanding, results in a security that brings quiet stability and sure trust even in the hardest of times.

7. **A great spotlight for right convictions**-Joshua 24:15. At the conclusion of his public ministry, Joshua with great conviction and determination thunders, "But as for me and my house, we will serve the Lord." Public ministry and private living combine to spotlight right convictions and a lifestyle that is powerful and believable to others.

8. **A great testimony of faithfulness**-1 Corinthians 4:2. Specifically Paul states that the chief requirement of stewardship is the attribute of faithfulness. In the wise managing and handling of our marriage relationship, the Lord requires the believing couple to be faithful. Remaining faithful to the Lord and to each other results in joy that is hard to express.

9. **A great safeguard**-Ecclesiastes 9:9. A "One husband and one wife, as long as life shall last" kind of joyfulness is a great safeguard against sinfulness and foolishness. The writer of Ecclesiastes reminds his readers that after trying everything imaginable, there is nothing like living joyfully with your wife all your life. This is great counsel for wise living.

10. **A great partnership**-1 Timothy 3:2. For those in pastoral positions, the phrase "The husband of one wife" is far more than simply making it through a lifetime without divorcing. Rather, the idea literally is expressed in the pastor so loving his wife that he actually becomes a one-woman kind of man.

    Becoming a one-woman kind of man and a one-man kind of woman is a wonderful blessing that results from a great marriage. This kind of partnership requires care and devotion as well as help from the Lord. It is a blessing indeed and one to be sought after with great diligence.

These ought to be the goals of every couple as they prepare for marriage. Throughout the counseling process, this supplement worksheet may be used for encouragement as well as instruction.

Help for Those Who Grew Up in a Troubled Home

Every couple has something in common with every other couple as they enter marriage. Though there are myriads of differences in the lives of the various soon-to-be-newlyweds, the one thing every couple shares in common is that they have a past. Wonderful lessons of blessings are part of the past that couples bring into their marriage. Memories can be great. But sometimes memories can haunt a person. There may be hurts, wounds, and scars that people carry with them into their wedding and married life.

Paul had a past in which things took place that he regretted. To Timothy, his dear son in the faith, he wrote, "And I thank Christ Jesus our Lord, who hath enabled me, for that he counted me faithful, putting me into the ministry; who was before a blasphemer, and a persecutor, and injurious…." (1 Timothy 1:12-13). Though Paul remembered these things, he rejoiced that these situations were past, dealt with in grace, and now by the mercy of God, he was moving forward in his look and life.

Sometimes our past holds far too much power, time and attention in our lives. To live the life the Lord desires for us, we must come to the place where we let our past be past. There are several precious things to lay hold of in this hope and help available.

The Blessings of a Biblical Family

The Key word is "biblical." There are no perfect families. A biblical family is one that truly desires to follow the Lord Jesus and obey His Word. It is a place where several key characteristics are consistent:

Safety-No one is intentionally belittled, humiliated, wounded, or hurt physically, emotionally, sexually, or spiritually.

Security-Home is a safe place where you know you belong. You are part of the family. That knowledge comes from being told, love that is shared, and acts that reinforce the statement, "You belong."

Individuality-You are different from your siblings; but they are not better and you are not inferior. Everyone has strengths and weaknesses. Your talents might not be identical to your siblings. However, you are accepted and loved for who you are. There is consistent encouragement to become the person God wants you to be.

Sense of worth-Your value is not in looks, ability, talent or achievement. The true sense of worth comes from the wonderful truth that God has begun a good work in you and will continue that great work (Philippians 1:6). As a believer, you are His workmanship (Ephesians 2:10) and a trophy of His grace (Ephesians 1:6). Your entire sense of worth comes from the grace of God and His wonderful work in your life.

Forgiveness- A biblical family is not perfect. Mistakes are made. Hurts happen. When a trespass or offence takes place, rather than offering excuses or blaming others, you experience repentance and sorrow for sin. Quickly you acknowledge this and, apologize to those that are hurt. Forgiveness is sought and you rejoice in the restoration of fellowship. When others hurt you, the same forgiveness is extended to them.

This forgiveness or cancellation of the indebtedness is not held over one another as a constant reminder. It is also not used as ammunition at a later time against each other. A biblical home is one in which the act of forgiveness is both learned and demonstrated by giving and receiving it.

Relationships nurtured and developed-Living in a specific location with parents and siblings provides a dynamic opportunity for you to connect with people who have different personalities, opinions and abilities. Relationship is all about connecting and being part of the life of another, even if that person is very different in personality from you.

Fun place to live-While not every moment is fun, exciting and adventuresome, a biblical home is one that makes it fun to be part of. You and your family look forward to coming home because it is a place marked by love, joy, peace, longsuffering, gentleness, goodness, faith, meekness and temperance. This is known as the fruit of the Spirit (Galatians 5:22-23). It is not perfect; but still, a biblical home is a great place to be.

Common Types of Troubled Homes

Abusive-This can be physical, emotional or sexual abuse.

Substance abuse-The common types of substance abuse include alcohol and illegal or misused prescription drugs.

Violent-There are various kinds and degrees of violence that take place in troubled homes. Sometimes the violence comes by threats and screaming; other times the physical violence happens in various degrees from pushing, to hitting, and even to homicide.

Deficient-In this troubled home, the very basic needs of life are ignored and unmet. Sick children are not taken to the doctor. On cold days, they are not properly clothed. Hungry children go to bed with little or no food in their home. Often funds that should be used to meet the basic needs of the family are spent unwisely or sinfully.

Domineering-The opposite extreme of deficient, the domineering home is one in which the child is nearly smothered by an overly involved parent or parents. In this home, the child has little or no opportunity for personal growth, alone time, or experimentation. A domineering parent demands exclusive involvement in every detail of the child's life.

Cold, harsh-An emotional distance with others is maintained by the unloving, cold, and insensitive family members. No emotional attachment or closeness is formed within this kind of family home. Years later, this adult looks back over his lifetime and again realizes the deep painfulness of never being told of a parent's love, appreciation, or affection.

Parental perfectionist-Living with a highly successful parent who has exceeding or nearly impossible expectations for the child is a wound waiting to happen. A perfectionist has very little grace or patience with others. Love is given as a reward for doing something perfectly. Even then, a particular deed or activity should have been just a little bit better.

Specific sins that become a pattern-While every person sins, there are sinful acts that become entrenched into a pattern of living. These include anger, worry, gossip, sexual immorality, covetousness, laziness, and a host of others. The Scriptures call us to be overcomers in Christ. This troubled home either is not saved or is falling short of the Lord's standards for godly living.

Common Characteristics of Those from a Troubled Home

Difficulty believing-If you grew up in such a home where one or more of the above things took place, it is very hard to believe that anyone would ever love you, especially God. You may think, "Why would God love me when my own family, who is supposed to love me, never did?"

No relationships-When basic family relationships were never nurtured or encouraged, it becomes very difficult later in life to form lasting and meaningful relationships with others. When promises are routinely broken, emotional attachment is severely limited, and blame is leveled at the one who is not responsible for the sinful situation, you may find yourself driven into a deep retreat and distrust for others. From this vantage point you probably think, "Trust no one; go it alone; don't make myself vulnerable. I will only get hurt." Isolation, bitter loneliness, and only the very shallowest of relationships are formed. Marriages suffer greatly because of this.

Approval-Frequently a person who has grown up in a very troubled home seeks approval by achievement and accomplishment. Often approval, even if it was very little and very infrequent, came only when earned by significant achievement. It is not uncommon if you are extremely driven to achieve, to acknowledge that this was your motivation and only means of approval ever experienced.

Actions hated-One of the amazing characteristics of those who grew up in a troubled home is that the actions of the parent, so hated by the child, now are being lived out through the adult child. Promising yourself that you would never do to others what your mother or father did to you, in an incredible and devastating way, today you act just like the person who hurt you. Unless the sinful pattern is broken, these actions hated as a child are often repeated later in life.

Fears and doubts-Lack of confidence is often the chief characteristic of those who grew up in troubled homes. Fears and doubts are the common emotions that plague people who have been constantly belittled, made fun of and ridiculed. Growing up in a troubled home sometimes results in such a poor image of self that some adults never overcome and live in persistent doubt and fear.

Confusion-Adults from troubled pasts often confuse people who try to love them. In fact, you may frequently confuse yourself. Inwardly you judge yourself so harshly; but outwardly as a defense mechanism you live with an attitude of superiority. Two different dynamics are taking place in your life. The inward turmoil and outward superiority are hard to cope with indeed.

How Do You Begin to Overcome the Hurts of the Past?

Believe God really has a plan for you. Regardless of the road you have traveled, in spite of what has happened to you, even though there are regrets, God still has a plan. He is can restore that which was lost, heal that which was wounded, and repair the greatest hurts and brokenness.

To the household of Israel in their deepest affliction and dispersion, the Lord assured them He has a plan. Jeremiah wrote, "For I know the thoughts that I think toward you, saith the LORD, thoughts of peace, and not of evil, to give you an expected end" (Jeremiah 29:11).

Remember, you are not alone. Often the person who grew up in a troubled home has feelings of shame, resentment, embarrassment and humiliation. Satan tries to convince you that no one else has ever experienced what you are going through. Isolation and withdrawing from others take place because you are sure that your horrible experience is unique to you alone.

The Lord assures us through the Apostle Paul, "There hath no temptation taken you but such as is common to man: but God is faithful, who will not suffer you to be tempted above that ye are able; but will with the temptation also make a way to escape, that ye may be able to bear it" (1 Corinthians 10: 13). You are not alone. Others have experienced the same things through which you have walked. The Lord has helped them to overcome. He will help you as well, if you will let Him.

Follow the directions. Simple, quick and easy formulas for overcoming do not produce lasting results. There are no quick fixes, even though we desire them. However, the Lord does provide us with very clear principles and directives that must be accepted and applied to your personal life. These disciplines must consistently become part of your life to overcome the hurts of a troubled past.

1. **Trust Christ for salvation** (2 Corinthians 5:17). This is the starting point for successful and blessed living.

2. **Be honest** with the Lord, yourself and others about your experience and feelings. Do not live in denial, pretending everything is fine if it is not (Ephesians 4:15).

3. **Specifically target the sinful patterns** in your own life. Recognize the areas that are displeasing to the Lord and confess them to Him (Ephesians 4:17). As a believer, be careful not to live the lifestyle or pattern of behavior a typical unsaved person lives. Do not offer excuses and do not blame others. Target areas that the Lord reveals are displeasing in your life, and ask the Lord to help you to begin to work on them.

4. **Think and live biblically** (Ephesians 4:23). You must make the Bible your personal standard for living. Do not live by feelings. Read it daily and accept its teaching as your guide. Regardless of how you might feel or what you might think, always make the Bible the final statement for your authority.

5. **Practice the "put off-put on" principle** of successful Christian living (Ephesians 4:22-24). Sinful actions and attitudes are to be confessed and put off as you would take off dirty or soiled clothing. In their place, with the Lord's help, put on actions and attitudes that are pleasing to Him. Specific sins confessed and forsaken and specific victories won by the Lord in the life of a surrendered believer are a joy to behold.

6. **Let your past be past** (Philippians 3:13). Everyone has a past. It is past. That's why it is called a past. Imagine the hazard that would occur if you drove twenty miles looking only in the rear view mirror. Most would not want to meet you on that highway. Likewise, those who live constantly in the past and wallow in their hurt and failure, never safely and happily negotiate the highway of relationships. In your marriage, this will be especially true.

7. **Cultivate the fruit of the Holy Spirit** (Galatians 5:22-23). As you mature and grow, and as the Word of God becomes more real and is applied in your daily life, the Holy Spirit begins to produce fruit that only He can grow. The nine-fold fruit of the Spirit demonstrates Christian living directed toward the Lord, others, and yourself.

These dynamic principles are not quick, nor are they easy. They are, however, God's specific steps for overcoming an unhappy past. Consistent and persistent application will produce godly living that does not exist by looking and living in the past. In a gracious way, you as a believer must accept by faith what God says and apply it to daily living. This will help your marriage to become truly blessed.

Chapter Fourteen
The Tests and Assignments

Through the handbook, the various tests and assignments are listed in the various counseling sessions. In some of the sessions, the tests are partially shared in the particular chapter. These are the tests and assignments that will be used as a supplement to the premarital counseling materials of the officiating pastor and may be duplicated for individual completion.

The tests and assignments are also found in the couple's edition and may be copied for individual completion. For the very best results, it is recommended that both the bride and groom purchase their own edition of *From This Day Forward—Couple's Edition*.

It will be helpful to remember that these tests and assignments are not exhaustive. They are designed to help the officiating pastor by supplementing his current premarital counseling ministry.

"Information Intake" is completed before the first premarital counseling session. This provides basic but important information for the first session.

"Respect and Priority" is assigned at the conclusion of counseling session 1 and provides the material for counseling session 2. The officiating pastor should require this homework to be completed and submitted to him at least two weeks before session 2 is scheduled.

"The Road Already Traveled" is a lengthy test which will be used in counseling sessions 3, 4 and 5 as well as the postmarital counseling follow-up. Some couples will work on this assignment for several weeks. Schedule plenty of time to adequately compare answers and see potential blessings as well as conflicts.

"Great Questions and Honest Answers" typically will be given at the conclusion of session 3, to be discussed in session 4. However, if the officiating pastor wishes, it may be given at any time during the premarital counseling process. The responses do not need to be returned unless the officiating pastor so desires. This assignment is specifically designed for the couple to become engaged in honest discussion and preparation for their married life. If a situation has not been resolved, it must be addressed in counseling.

"Our Financial Planner" is to be given at the conclusion of chapter 3 and will be used in session 4. This is a basic planner and is very suitable for most soon-to-be-married couples.

"The Journey of Ron and Lisa" will be assigned at the conclusion of session 4 and will be addressed in session 5. This will be in addition to any areas of concern that surface from the test "The Road Already Traveled."

"Our Wedding" provides the information and specific details of the wedding, special features and participants. This will be especially helpful to the officiating pastor on the night of the wedding rehearsal. All the details are instantly available in this resource.

"Now That We Are Married" is designed to help the couple prepare for the six-month postwedding ceremony session. This should be submitted to the officiating pastor at least two weeks before the postmarital counseling session. "The Road Already Traveled," Section 10 is also used in this session.

Information Intake—*Introducing Ourselves*

Bride's Information:

Bride's full name _____

Address _____

Date of birth _____ Home phone _____

Cell phone _____

Status: Is this your first marriage? _____

Are you a member of a local church? _____

Name of church _____

Family background:

Names of parents _____

Names and ages of siblings _____

_____

Do you have a personal relationship with the Lord Jesus Christ? _____

If yes, please write a brief paragraph of your testimony of salvation. ___

_____

_____

_____

_____

What are several of the goals for premarital counseling you wish the pastor to emphasize? ___

_____

_____

_____

_____

Are you committed to six (may vary) sessions of premarital counseling
and the completion of homework assignments before each appointment? _____

Date of proposed wedding _____

Location of proposed wedding _____

Chapter 14

Information Intake—*Introducing Ourselves*

Groom's Information:

Groom's full name _____

Address _____

Date of birth _____ Home phone _____

Cell phone _____

Status: Is this your first marriage? _____

Are you a member of a local church? _____

Name of church _____

Family background:

Names of parents _____

Names and ages of siblings _____

_____

Do you have a personal relationship with the Lord Jesus Christ? _____

If yes, please write a brief paragraph of your testimony of salvation. ____

_____

_____

_____

_____

What are several of the goals for premarital counseling you wish the pastor to emphasize? _____

_____

_____

_____

Are you committed to six (may vary) sessions of premarital counseling and the completion of homework assignments before each appointment? _____

Respect and Priority

Homework for Pre-Marital Counseling Session 2

Respect is the demonstration of appreciation that we have for our future mate. Priority demonstrates what is important to us. Both respect and priority are essential to healthy marriages.

The Story of Mark and Mindy

> Mark and Mindy arrived for their premarital counseling appointment with nervousness and anticipation. They were to be married in less than six months and this would potentially be one of the most important moments in their lives.
>
> Mark grew up in a home where fighting and friction became part of daily living. Neither of Mark's parents are believers and both mom and dad were demanding and self-centered. While the fighting seldom was physical, the damage was severe. Mark's mother has never worked outside the home. She views her husband as a failure who never measured up to her expectations. Often she would complain that they needed more money. Mark's dad became more and more withdrawn and seemed to find his fulfillment through his work. He worked more hours, came home less frequently and though they made more money, the home became more tense and unhappy. They divorced each other four years before Mark and Mindy became engaged.
>
> Mindy's family are believers. Her mom is a career woman. She has taught in the same elementary school since she graduated from college. Dad owns and operates his own business. Both are supportive of each other's careers. Both are very active in their local church. Mom teaches children, and dad is an usher and treasurer. Mom is a conversationalist and very much wants to talk with her husband about everything. She teases him that after spending all day with third graders, she would like to talk with an adult. Dad is a very gracious man and often compliments his wife. They love to talk with each other and are faithful in their devotions. Their home, while not perfect, is warm, loving, respectful, and spiritually minded.

This is the background of Mark and Mindy. Based on this information, in your own words, please answer the following questions.

1. Knowing that our values and impressions of marriage are caught from watching our parents, how would you express the picture of marriage Mark and Mindy mostly likely have when it comes to marriage?

Mark's picture: _____

_____

_____

Mindy's picture: _____

_____

_____

Chapter 14

2. What were the obvious priorities in the families of both Mark and Mindy?

Mark's family: _____

_____

_____

Mindy's family: _____

_____

_____

3. How would you counsel Mark and Mindy concerning the right priorities to begin establishing in their marriage, based on their pictures? _____

_____

_____

_____

_____

4. How were respect and priority communicated in the home in which you grew up? _____

_____

_____

_____

5. What are the ways your future mate communicates respect and priority to you? _____

_____

_____

_____

6. How do you communicate respect and priority to your future mate? _____

_____

_____

_____

_____

The Road Already Traveled

Homework for Pre-Marital Counseling Sessions 3-5
Post-Marital

Name _____

The information you are sharing will be held in strict confidence. Your pastor/counselor greatly desires to assist you in preparing for your marriage and home by helping you to understand your background. You have been traveling a road that has brought you to the point in life where the strong points can be strengthened and weak areas identified and changed before you enter marriage.

Please answer these questions by using a scale of 1 to 4.
   1= Very strongly disagree, as this almost never describes my situation.
   2= Mildly disagree, as this usually does not describe my situation.
   3= Mildly agree, as this sometimes describes my situation.
   4= Strongly agree, as this describes my situation.

1. How I view marriage as modeled before me

_____ 1. I had the privilege of a close relationship with at least one set of grandparents.

_____ 2. I had the privilege of knowing my grandparents were happily married.

_____ 3. My grandparents were role models of how a happy marriage works.

_____ 4. I would describe my parents as happily married.

_____ 5. My parents openly express their love for each other.

_____ 6. I have frequently witnessed my parents being affectionate with each other.

_____ 7. My parents love the Lord and our home. Though not perfect, it is a model of what I would like my home to be.

_____ 8. I know the role of being a spiritual leader because it was consistently modeled in our home.

_____ 9. Family time in reading the Bible and praying was common in my home.

_____ 10. I remember great times spent together as a family in doing things together as well as special times on vacation.

2. How I view my relationship with the Lord

_____ 1. I know the Lord as my personal Savior and seek to live for Him.

_____ 2. I want to know and do the will of God because it provides great priorities in my life.

_____ 3. I read the Bible on a nearly daily basis.

_____ 4. I am a member of a Bible-believing church.

_____ 5. I have a regular ministry in my church.

_____ 6. I can honestly say my future mate and I agree on the importance of living for Christ and both of us are seeking to live for Him.

_____ 7. I have witnessed my future mate reading the Bible, praying and serving in some area of Christian service in our local church.

_____ 8. I am encouraged that my future mate is consistent in praying with me on a regular basis.

_____ 9. I can honestly say my future mate and I talk regularly about spiritual matters.

_____ 10. I know my future mate is growing spiritually and is becoming a mature disciple of the Lord Jesus Christ.

3. How I view things relating to my future home and marriage

_____ 1. My future mate and I have a strong relationship of trust and mutual respect.

_____ 2. My future mate and I have talked about finances and budgeting, and we are in agreement with how our finances will be handled.

_____ 3. My future mate and I have talked about the things that make a marriage strong.

_____ 4. My future mate has a good relationship with his or her parents.

_____ 5. I have a good relationship with my parents.

_____ 6. My future mate and I have talked about the relationship we wish to have with both sets of parents after we are married.

_____ 7. My future mate and I agree on tithing and regular giving to the local church.

_____ 8. My future mate and I have talked about parenting and how to raise children.

_____ 9. My future mate and I are in agreement with the number of children we would like to have.

_____ 10. My future mate and I are in agreement with how we would like to spend holidays and vacations.

4. My current situation

_____ 1. Financially, I live within my means and adhere to a budget.

_____ 2. Financially, my mate lives within his/her means and adheres to a budget.

_____ 3. My future mate and I have a good level of communication and I am satisfied with it.

_____ 4. I feel like I can talk with my future mate about anything and will have his/her attention and understanding.

_____ 5. My future mate and I are currently serving the Lord in some capacity.

In this section, simply check the statements that best describe you.

5. My walk with the Lord

_____ I know the Lord as Savior

_____ I sometimes doubt my salvation

_____ I struggle with the assurance of salvation

_____ I am growing in my spiritual life

_____ I read the Bible nearly daily

_____ I pray throughout the day

_____ I am assured my future mate knows the Lord as personal Savior

_____ I grew up in a Christian home

_____ I am the first Christian in my family

_____ My future mate and I pray regularly together

_____ My future mate and I agree on the church in which we will be members

_____ My mate and I agree on how frequently we will attend our local church

_____ My mate and I enjoy serving in our local church

_____ The Lord has first priority in my life

6. Which of the following statements best describe you?

_____ Outgoing, friendly	_____ Humorous, funny	_____ Enjoys meeting people
_____ Talkative	_____ Enthusiastic	_____ Generous
_____ Undisciplined	_____ Disorganized	_____ Exaggerates at times
_____ Can be insensitive	_____ Cold, unsympathetic	_____ Hostile, angry
_____ Unforgiving	_____ Domineering	_____ Opinionated
_____ Proud	_____ Productive	_____ Practical, logical
_____ Self-confident	_____ Calm, quiet	_____ Easygoing
_____ Diplomatic	_____ Dependable	_____ Reluctant leader
_____ Unmotivated	_____ Stubborn	_____ Indecisive
_____ Fearful	_____ Analytical	_____ Perfectionist
_____ Sensitive	_____ Self-sacrificing	_____ Moody
_____ Critical	_____ Revengeful	_____ Very loving

7. **Which of the following statements best describe your future mate?**

_____ Outgoing, friendly	_____ Humorous, funny	_____ Enjoys meeting people
_____ Talkative	_____ Enthusiastic	_____ Generous
_____ Undisciplined	_____ Disorganized	_____ Exaggerates at times
_____ Can be insensitive	_____ Cold, unsympathetic	_____ Hostile, angry
_____ Unforgiving	_____ Domineering	_____ Opinionated
_____ Proud	_____ Productive	_____ Practical, logical
_____ Self-confident	_____ Calm, quiet	_____ Easygoing
_____ Diplomatic	_____ Dependable	_____ Reluctant leader
_____ Unmotivated	_____ Stubborn	_____ Indecisive
_____ Fearful	_____ Analytical	_____ Perfectionist
_____ Sensitive	_____ Self-sacrificing	_____ Moody
_____ Critical	_____ Revengeful	_____ Very loving

8. **Which of the statements best describe the home in which you grew up?**

_____ I was an only child	_____ Godly father	_____ Godly mother
_____ Spiritually-minded home	_____ Warm, loving	_____ Love demonstrated
_____ Fun, laughter	_____ Generally happy home	_____ People visited often
_____ Devotions together	_____ Cold, unloving	_____ Harsh, demanding
_____ Perfectionist demands	_____ Spontaneous	_____ Quiet, lonely at times
_____ Often noisy, activities	_____ Organized, orderly	_____ Well-disciplined
_____ Too permissive	_____ Too disciplined	_____ Favoritism shown
_____ Good parenting	_____ Regular vacations	_____ All shared chores
_____ Talked together	_____ Ignored problems	_____ Resolved problems
_____ Generous	_____ Often had at least one meal together daily	
_____ Respect shown	_____ Respect taught consistently	

9. **Which of the statements best describe the home in which your future partner grew up?**

_____ I was an only child	_____ Godly father	_____ Godly mother
_____ Spiritually-minded home	_____ Warm, loving	_____ Love demonstrated

110 *From This Day Forward*

_____ Fun, laughter　　_____ Generally happy home　　_____ People visited often

_____ Devotions together　　_____ Cold, unloving　　_____ Harsh, demanding

_____ Perfectionist demands　　_____ Spontaneous　　_____ Quiet, lonely at times

_____ Often noisy, activities　　_____ Organized, orderly　　_____ Well-disciplined

_____ Too permissive　　_____ Too disciplined　　_____ Favoritism shown

_____ Good parenting　　_____ Regular vacations　　_____ All shared chores

_____ Talked together　　_____ Ignored problems　　_____ Resolved problems

_____ Generous　　_____ Often had at least one meal together daily

_____ Respect shown　　_____ Respect taught consistently

10. Complete the following statements in your own words

A. When I think about marriage, I feel- _____

_____

_____

_____

_____

B. Some of the things I appreciate about my future mate include- _____

_____

_____

_____

_____

C. Among my expectations in marriage, several that are very important to me include- _____

_____

_____

_____

_____

D. Several areas that need to improve in my life would include- _____
_____
_____
_____
_____

Several areas that need to improve in the life of my future mate would include- _____
_____
_____
_____
_____

E. When I think of the number of children I would like to have it would be- _____
_____
_____
_____
_____

F. When I think of the ideal way of spending an evening together with my future mate, it would be-
_____
_____
_____
_____

G. When I think of the ideal vacation, it would be- _____
_____
_____
_____
_____

Perhaps there are areas of concern or questions that this homework has not addressed. Please feel free to list these or any other statement you wish to communicate to the pastor/counselor.

Let's Share- Great Questions and Honest Answers

To Be Reviewed for Session 4

1. How do you see our careers impacting our marriage both in good and in possibly difficult ways?
2. What are our individual goals relating to our careers?
3. How long do we want to wait before trying to have a baby?
4. How many children would we hope to have someday?
5. What if one of us is ready to begin our family and the other is not? How will we resolve this?
6. What will some of the changes be in our home and personal lives when the Lord allows us to have a child?
7. Are we agreed as to the method of birth control we want to use? Have we worked through this sufficiently in our minds after receiving good counsel from our physician and pastor? Are we sure this method prevents pregnancy and does not terminate it?
8. What are our plans as relating to housing? Which will work best for us right now, renting or purchasing a home?
9. How large a place do we think we really need right now?
10. How much of our income should we spend on housing? If we are not sure, are we willing to discuss this with our pastor in the premarital counseling time?
11. How important is money in our relationship?
12. What are three or four material possessions we would like to acquire someday that will require savings and a significant investment?
13. How do we define financial security?
14. What should be our attitude about indebtedness?
15. How many credit cards should we have?
16. How important should it be to pay off the balance on our credit card or cards every month?
17. Should we have a joint checking account, or should we have separate accounts?
18. How much should we save each month, and how we will invest our savings?
19. Even though retirement is a long way off, how much should we invest in our retirement account? How much should we tuck away in an emergency fund?
20. What are some of the things we will enjoy doing together around the house?
21. Will we grocery shop together? If not, whose responsibility should this be?
22. Who will be responsible for cooking? Will we share this responsibility together and if so, how?
23. What about household chores? How will we share in these?
24. How often would we enjoy eating out?
25. How important is dating after we are married?
26. How often will we go out with our friends?
27. How often will we entertain friends in our home?

28. What are some of the good things we appreciate in the home and marriage of our parents which we would like to bring into our home and marriage?
29. What are some things we would like to change and incorporate into our home and marriage?
30. What are some of the possible conflicts that might arise out of our personality differences? How will we deal with these possibilities?
31. How will we handle holidays with our families?
32. How we will handle vacations?
33. How will we work through conflicts without hurting each other?
34. What place will the Lord hold in our home and marriage?
35. How important are daily worship and prayer as individuals and as a couple?
36. What will be our local church?
37. How important will it be in our marriage for us to serve the Lord?
38. If someday a missions trip should become a possibility, would we be willing to prayerfully consider going together?
39. What does a healthy marriage look like to us?
40. What does the role of a good husband look like? What does the role of a good wife look like?
41. What do we think a healthy sexual relationship seems to be?
42. How often do we hope to have sex in a typical week?
43. How will we handle it when one is interested in having sex and the other is not?
44. How much do we honestly understand about the difference between the way a man views sex and the way a woman's view of sex?
45. How will we make big decisions together?
46. What if we discover someday that we cannot have children? Would we ever be willing to consider adoption?
47. What do you really appreciate about me? What are some areas that I really need to be working on?
48. Why do you want to marry me?
49. Would we be willing to speak with our pastor and go for marriage counseling if someday we encounter a situation we cannot resolve ourselves?
50. What are several major safeguards we want to establish to make sure our marriage stays healthy and grows throughout our lifetime?

Couples should not tackle all the questions at one sitting. Allow each other the privilege of being honest. Understand that this is how each one views the situation at this time. Work though the questions and speak freely, carefully, graciously and forthrightly.

If there are questions that cannot be resolved at this time, mark the question or questions. Commit to each other that you will pray about them and if they are still unresolved, you will take these matters to the next premarital counseling session to work through it with the pastor.

Our Financial Planner For Session 4

Monthly Income

Gross Monthly Income .... _____

Investment Income .... _____

Total Monthly Income .... _____

Monthly Deductions

Tithe and Offering .... _____

Federal Income Tax .... _____

State/Local Taxes .... _____

Social Security/Medicare .... _____

Total Monthly Gross Income .... _____

Total Monthly Tithe/ Taxes .... _____

Total Remaining Usable Monthly Income _____

Expenses: Housing Costs

Mortgage/ Rent .... _____

Homeowners/ Renters Insurance ..... _____

Property Taxes .... _____

Repairs/Improvements .... _____

Utilities:

Electric .... _____   Gas .... _____

Water/Sewer _____   Telephone _____

Total Housing Expenses _____

Expenses: Food and Grocery .... _____

Expenses: Heath Insurance Medical Expenses .... _____

Expenses: Transportation

Car payment .... _____

Insurance .... _____

Gas/oil/repairs .... _____

Miscellaneous tolls/parking .... _____

Total Transportation _____

Expenses: Credit Cards/Loans .... _____

Expenses: Entertainment / Recreation / Personal .... _____

Savings/ Investments .... _____

Total Monthly Usable Income _____

Total Monthly Projected Expenses _____

Current Status (Positive or Negative) _____

Chapter 14

The Journey of Ron and Lisa

Homework for Pre-Marital Counseling Session 5

"Getting to Know the Real Me"

Ron and Lisa have been married for thirteen years. Though they grew up in the same general area in the rural farming lands of Iowa, their backgrounds are very different. As you read their story of their marriage journey, think through the importance of understanding your mate as well as yourself.

Ron's family were hard-working farmers who seldom took time off as they worked from before dawn until late in the day, almost every day. Ron's mom and dad were young children when their individual families moved to Iowa to work the land. Five brothers and three sisters caused Ron's life to be filled with noise, laughter and times of rivalry that caused mom to swat the children with a rolled up towel! "Out of my kitchen and stop that racket" often were the words mom shouted in good nature and with a smile as she scooted the children on their way.

The Lord was the center of the life of Ron's family. Though the farm required many hours every day, the Lord was honored early in the morning. Individually each member of the family had quiet moments in the Word of God and prayer. Breakfast took place together after dad had already worked several hours. No food was served until dad carefully took the old family Bible off the shelf in the kitchen and carefully brought it to the table. The atmosphere was not harsh or rigid. However, each child knew this was not the time to wiggle or giggle. Dad read a portion of the Word and one of the children would be asked to lead in prayer and thank the Lord for the day and the food. As soon as the "Amen" was spoken, all quietness and serenity were shattered as massive amounts of food were passed and most of the family talked at the same time.

Immediately after supper, as soon as the dishes were taken to the sink, the family gathered in the living room of Ron's old farm house for what was called "evening worship." Ron's mom often played a hymn or two on the old upright piano. Even though it was not in tune and even though the family was not composed of great singers, wonderful times of music and worship took place around that old piano. Dad would often read from the Bible and then make up a story of his own that would illustrate what the family read.

The children grew older and one by one left the home for college or marriage. The family circle grew smaller. Ron, who was number six in the line of nine children, was old enough to remember the great evenings of large family gathering in a small living room. Even better were the times when guests were present and everything stopped for "evening worship." By the time Ron was preparing for marriage, the family gatherings were half the size; but they were precious still in the learning of God's ways and growing as a family of believers.

Ron had a personality that was very outgoing. He loved to meet people and conversation came easily for him. As Ron would be sent into town on an errand, dad would often remind him, "Ronnie, get back here with the tractor part as soon as you can. Don't stop and talk with everyone you meet." Ron would laugh and wave to his dad as he jumped into his rusty pickup that had over 314,000 miles on it. Dust from the driveway flew as Ron headed to town eagerly waiting who he might see at the parts supply store.

Everyone seemed to love Ron's sense of humor and generosity. He was funny; but still had a concern for others that was demonstrated by his impulsive willingness to share. Sometimes Ron gave away most of his paycheck because someone else had a need. Later, there would be a time or two when he would have trouble paying a bill because with little or no thought of his own needs, he gave away a large part of his paycheck.

Enthusiasm was second nature to Ron. Nothing daunted him. He awoke long before the alarm would go off. Eager and excited about the day, Ron often annoyed the two other brothers who shared the room but did not share the same outlook. By the time the alarm would sound, Ron had already thought of two jokes, ten questions and fifteen things to talk about. The other two brothers were simply trying to remember where they were and what day it was! Pillows often flew at Ron as the other brothers covered their heads with their blankets.

Ron had a hard time understanding why others were not as cheerful and excited about life. Lisa had noticed Ron on several occasions. He was always talking with someone and frequently would end the conversation with laughter and a gentle slap on the shoulder of the other men as he left the group. She would not be noticed by Ron until Lisa's family visited the church where Ron and his family attended. Right in the middle of the hymn Ron glanced in Lisa's direction and spotted her. There, right before his eyes, was the most beautiful young woman he had even seen. Ron didn't get very much out of the service that Sunday. Though Ron had often been accused of exaggerating, this time he really meant it when he whispered to himself, "She is the most incredibly beautiful woman I have ever seen." The service could not end fast enough for Ron that Sunday. Several were surprised that Ron didn't speak in return to them as he flew past six pews of worshippers to meet the beautiful, but very shy and introverted, Lisa.

She spotted him coming. It would be no exaggeration to say she could feel her face starting to burn as she knew it was turning red. Oh, to stop that blushing! Why does it always come at the worst time in the world" she thought. Ron introduced himself and began to talk non-stop. His normal extroverted personality seemed in overdrive as he talked with the visitor named Lisa.

Lisa's family lived in the neighboring town about twenty miles from Ron and his family. Hard work was a normal part of their lives but farming was not the family business. Lisa's dad was a professor in a local community college and her mother taught in the elementary school in town. Lisa was the oldest of the sibling group of three daughters. She and her family were close and enjoyed doing things together.

Lisa's personality was very quiet, calm and easygoing. Often she heard her parents talk about the need to find a church somewhere, sometime. She never pressed the issue, assuming that sooner or later they would get around to it. Studies came fairly easy to Lisa. That was a huge blessing, because Lisa often would procrastinate in many areas, including her school work. Even though mom and dad were in public education, Lisa had the attitude of "When it comes to term papers, why start today what could be started tomorrow?"

There were times of tension in the family between her parents and Lisa as mom and dad did not share this same viewpoint. Though she was a procrastinator, Lisa was very dependable. She was never early in completing an assignment; but she was consistently on time. She was totally dependable in other areas as well. Seldom did Lisa miss an obligation or fail to keep a promise.

Probably the most difficult thing in the world for Lisa was to make decisions. One of the reasons she would procrastinate on her term papers was found in trying to decide the subject for her writing. This difficulty in making decisions translated into most areas of her life. Many times her sisters would become impatient with her as they waited for her to decide what sweater to wear or what color slacks to select. Several times she was left behind because she was having trouble making up her mind again.

Lisa's family had very little interest in spiritual things. That started to change when a good friend died suddenly as the result of a tragic automobile accident. Lisa's family was deeply moved at the funeral service conducted by Pastor Winters. They were impressed by his gentle and loving remarks. His message directly from the Bible was amazing and something brand new to them. However, it was the loving and caring congregation of the church who reached out to the family of the deceased friend that convinced Lisa's family that something big was missing in their lives. Whatever this congregation had, Lisa's family needed.

Two weeks later, during an appointment Lisa's dad made with Pastor Winters, Lisa's family together placed their faith in Christ. Pastor Winter's could not remember the last time he led an entire family to the Lord. Lisa's family would visit Pastor Winters's church the next Sunday.

True to form, while everyone else was very nervous about this new activity for Sunday morning, Lisa was even keeled and collected. The hardest part of the entire morning for her was to decide between her yellow dress and the pink outfit which was given to her for her last birthday. The rest of the family headed for the car when she finally decided on the yellow outfit. Dad had to hurry to keep from being late. She noticed Ron that first Sunday but was too shy to hardly look up when he and a group of friends walked nearby.

It was on the second visit that Ron had discovered her. As they dated they truly enjoyed getting to know each other. Lisa found Ron amusing, funny, and animated, never running out of good stories or sharing news of things that were going on in his life. Lisa was so easy to date. She seldom had a preference as to where they would eat a bite of lunch together. Ron did notice that she seemed to have a hard time deciding even on little things on the menu. She was a good calming influence, in his life and he encouraged her to be a little more outgoing. A year later they were engaged, and six months later they married.

Now thirteen years and two children ages 9 and 6 later, Ron and Lisa are making an appointment for marriage counseling. Pastor Winters has retired; but their current Pastor has scheduled an intake session to gather information and data about Ron and Lisa.

Ron has told the pastor, "I love my wife, but she never gets around to anything. She has unfinished projects all over the house. I don't think she even loves me anymore. She never is affectionate. She is unresponsive to me in every way. And stubborn-I want to tell you pastor, is she ever stubborn!"

Through her tears, Lisa said, "Pastor, I can see why my husband feels this way. But he has pushed me away. He makes promises he does not keep. He has forgotten both my birthday and our anniversary. He talks; but never stops to listen. In fact, he is always talking, talking, talking; but never listening. We are behind in our bills because Ron has insisted on helping his sister and her family. I am sorry they are out of work; but we have bills too. When I tried to tell him I was concerned about this, he made a joke about it and gave them additional funds. I really don't think my husband loves us. He is always running here and there to help everyone else."

As the bridal couple, imagine you are the counseling pastor.

1. What are several key characteristics of Ron's personality? _____

2. What are several key characteristics of Lisa's personality? _____

3. What are several key areas in which the two different personalities complement each other? _____

4. What are several key areas in which the two different personalities clash? _____

5. What are several key characteristics of your personality? _____

6. What are several key characteristics of your future mate's personality? _____

7. What are several ways your personalities complement each other? What are several ways your personalities clash? _____

Wedding Details for the Couple and Pastor

Groom's full name _____

Bride's full name _____

Date of wedding _____ Time _____

Maid/Matron of Honor _____

Maids attending _____

_____

_____

Best Man _____

Ushers _____

_____

_____

Flower Girl _____

Ring Bearer _____

Organist _____

Special music _____

_____

Wedding service selected _____

Wedding Coordinator _____

Florist _____

Photographer _____

Date of wedding rehearsal _____ Time _____

Approximate number attending wedding _____

Special features to be included in the ceremony _____

_____

_____

Master of Ceremonies at reception _____

From This Day Forward

Now That We Are Married

Post-Marital Follow Up Counseling

My name _____

List three things for which you are thankful in your marriage _____

_____

_____

List three things you appreciate about your mate _____

_____

_____

Use a scale of 1 to 5 to answer the following questions.
- 1= Very dissatisfied and very concerned, needs immediate attention.
- 2= Dissatisfied and concerned, we need to work on this.
- 3= All right, but surely could improve.
- 4= Satisfied with this situation and appreciate this blessing
- 5= Very satisfied and thank the Lord for this and will not take it for granted.

Mark the appropriate number by circling it for your answer. Place an X over the number you believe will be your partner's level of satisfaction. Please do not work on this together. Work separately and prayerfully on your answers.

1. The state of our walk with the Lord as a couple
    1 2 3 4 5

2. The routine we are developing in reading the Bible and praying together
    1 2 3 4 5

3. Our involvement in our local church   1 2 3 4 5

4. The daily time invested in talking with each other   1 2 3 4 5

5. The quality of free time we have to spend with each on a regular basis
    1 2 3 4 5

6. The amount of time we are apart from each other because of work and other activities   1 2 3 4 5

7. The way we are managing our money   1 2 3 4 5

8. The way we are adjusting to each other   1 2 3 4 5

9. The way we are making decisions together   1 2 3 4 5

10. The way we are managing conflicts when differing opinions surface   1 2 3 4 5

11. Our sexual interaction with each other   1 2 3 4 5

> Those two very good illustrations of the bank and the lawn really apply now. To have a healthy bank account, more deposits must be made than withdrawals. To have a healthy marriage, make far more investments than withdrawals. To have a healthy lawn, it takes work and care. The same is true with a healthy marriage.

12. Our level of involvement with friends and doing things with other couples   1 2 3 4 5

13. My spouse's relationship with my parents   1 2 3 4 5

14. My relationship with my spouse's parents   1 2 3 4 5

15. The level of satisfaction with my marriage   1 2 3 4 5

What are some of the situations you wish to discuss with the pastor? _____

_____

_____

During the premarital counseling process, the couple completed the lengthy test "The Road Already Traveled." Section 10 is completed now and will be compared with the answers given earlier.

Complete the following statements in your own words.

A. When I think about marriage, I feel- _____

_____

_____

_____

B. Some of the things I appreciate about my future mate include- _____

_____

_____

_____

C. Among my expectations in marriage, several that are very important to me include- _____

_____

_____

_____

D. Several areas that need to improve in my life would include- _____

_____

_____

_____

Several areas that need to improve in the life of my future mate would include- _____

_____

_____

_____

E. When I think of the number of children I would like to have, it would be-_____

F. When I think of the ideal way of spending an evening together with my mate, it would be-

G. When I think of the ideal vacation, it would be-_____

Other Resources by Dr. Michael Peck

From This Day Forward-Preparing Couples for the Journey of a Lifetime-Couple's Edition. This resource complements the counselor's edition in preparing engaged couples for a lifetime marriage. Couples will enjoy the detailed information in easy reading and practical application.

Steps of Joy-Preparing for Membership in My Local Church is available for the adult instructor and student. Ten lessons prepare men and women to become strong and godly members of their local church.

Steps of Joy for Boys and Girls prepares children to become members of the local church. A special feature of this resource is the "S-W-A-P," which means, a "Story With a Purpose." Written from the perspective of the child, biblical principles are clearly identified.

Discovering and Developing Leaders is available in both the instructor and student editions as well as DVD presentation. Future leaders must be found and developed in local churches through the Scriptures and a practical plan.

Be watching for additional resources on leadership development as well as marriage and parenting. These resources may be purchased online at www.bcpusa.org